FLYING HIGH
in a Polka Dot Dress

Olayemi A. Adelekan

Dedication

This book is dedicated to my father,
Elijah Bayode,
a man who gave his best to his family
and everyone he came across.

Acknowledgement

I would like to acknowledge my siblings, Segun, Tale and Toyin for their enthusiastic support when I pitched the initial idea for this book and for their stories. Many thanks to Toyin who had nearly as much passion for the book as I did and read through multiple versions of the manuscript.

Also I would like to acknowledge Adeniyi and Kemi – without them our family would not be complete.

Special thanks to my mum, Janet, who was always by my father's side and to Mr Olufe, his childhood friend, who acted as a life buoy to a drowning boy and became his best friend for life.

Also special thanks to Xenia Thompson, my editor, who handled this project with dedication and passion.

Mostly, my thanks to my father, without whom this book would not have been possible, and to my husband, Matthew, and sons, Matthew Jr. and Deji, for their unwavering love, understanding and support.

Foreword

I grew up with a father who found ways to inspire me every day.

- He learnt so he could teach me.
- He went without so I could have.
- He cried so I could laugh.
- He endured so I wouldn't have to.

The first two books I could remember him buying for my brother and I, were the 'Power of Positive Thinking" and "A Guide to Confident Living" by Dr Norman Vincent Peale. Both of us were still in primary school and my first thought, as a six or seven year old, was that there were no pictures in the book. I turned page after page wondering, 'where are the pictures?'

From then on, he never stopped looking for ways to educate and inspire us.

He died when I was only thirty-one and, ever since, not a week has gone by without me applying one of his lessons to my life or sharing them with others, to help them.

One thing I regularly get is people telling me how inspired they are by the stories I tell them. For every person who has been positively affected by my father or by one of the tales, I know there are millions more who could do with hearing them.

The day I decided to write this book was the day I envisioned all the people who needed to read the stories. In my mind's eye, I could see the orphans, the single parents, the abused children, the forgotten ones, the ones without hope, the parents who want to do better and those struggling to see a great future for their children.

Once I saw this, I knew I had to put all fear of failure aside and retell the stories as best as I could. I truly pray that their light will guide everyone who reads them

Olayemi A. Adelekan
Eli's daughter

I have been driven many times upon my knees by the overwhelming conviction that I had nowhere else to go. My own wisdom, and that of all about me, seemed insufficient for the day.

Lincoln, Abraham

I learn that sometimes even the termites have their own plans and you could do with knowing in plenty of time or at least having someone in your corner.

My dad grew up caring for himself from a very young age. I remember, he often told us, that at the time he started to fend for himself as a young child, he did not know that he needed to pull his trousers up when walking through a puddle, so his trousers would get *wet*.

By the time he was able to start his primary school education, he was old enough to get a girl pregnant. This was because he had to work and save money for his own school uniform, shoes, books and stationeries and as a child who ran errands and assisted in manual labour to make this money, it took him years to save up enough. This was despite the fact that both of his 'fathers – biological and step father' had enough money to send him to school but none of them chose to pay for him and his mum also chose to do nothing or could not afford to.

Dad often said that even though he had a roof over his head, he never quite knew where his meals would come from. Fortunately he made a friend and they got really close, going everywhere and doing everything together.

This friendship was a "God-send", as my father's survival would depend on it for many years to come. It was like a life buoy to a drowning man and his friend truly became an anchor for my dad: it led to a load of antics and endured right till his death.

My dad had most of his dinners at his friend's house and this became the only sure meal of any given day for him. His friend insisted that an extra portion had to be added to his own meal so that he could share it with my dad and often he would wait for him to come round, or go look for him if he was late, just so they could eat whatever was available.

My father only went home under the cover of night, slipped in unobtrusively and left in the morning before anyone noticed or picked on him, reminding him of how unwelcome he was in his own home.

Together my dad and his friend laboured and worked to save money for their school fees and anything else they wanted or needed. They did any job that was on offer, including manual labour on farms and construction sites. They had their own farm plots and ran any errands that they could get paid for.

They put aside most of their money towards their education, and had some adventures and life experiences along the way.

One of those experiences happened when they saved up for months to buy a new set of clothes for Christmas. In those days, if you were lucky and your parents could afford it, you would get three sets of new clothes every year: for the Easter, Christmas and New Year celebrations. My dad had no one to go to for new clothes and his friend's parents couldn't afford to buy them for their son.

They both came up with a plan to work and buy their own clothes and it was successfully put into action; they saved up, bought the fabrics and got a tailor to make their new outfits. Once they were ready, the boys stored away the clothes, waiting for Christmas day when they would show case – or more like show off – a year's worth of labour.

My dad and his friend made Christmas plans but so did the termites: they plotted to eat the clothes and took immediate action. When my dad and his friend went to get their new attire out from the wooden suitcase where they had been put for safe-keeping, all they found were tattered pieces of leftover fabric, yet to be fully eaten.

Absolutely nothing could be salvaged and, my father said, he and his friend both broke down and cried for ages. With no back up plans, no extra funds and no parents who cared or could afford to replace the clothes, they had an extremely disappointing and miserable Christmas.

As they were two young boys, who just saw a year's worth of labour go down the drain, this experience would leave a permanent imprint on both of them for years to come.

Growing up I noticed that my father wore whatever he bought on the same day and we often made fun of him when he would leave his old shoes in the store and wear the new ones home. The same thing happened with any new clothes – he wore them as soon as he bought them. Whenever my mum ordered him a new set of work suits, if there were five, he would wear them for the next five working days.

As children, my brother and I could never understand his rationale until my dad told us the story about the termites eating his new clothes. That experience meant that my father never had 'Sunday-best' clothes; he wore and enjoyed whatever he had as soon as he had it. I guess that, as a child, he swore never to delay the gratification of enjoying what he had worked for. Or perhaps he just never wanted the termites to get the better of him ever again.

In the end it was Termites: 1, Daddy: countless wins.

So my dad won in the end, enjoying every victory for the rest of his life. Because of this experience he lived his life to the fullest, capitalising on every opportunity and enjoying every reward that came his way.

Most of the important things in the world have been accomplished by people who have kept on trying when there seemed to be no hope at all.

Carnegie, Dale

I learn about having the audacity to ask – daddy asks to be considered for an all girls' school, proving that if you want something badly enough, you will find a way to make it happen.

When I thought of writing this book, I was spurred on because, each time I told a story about my father, I saw friends, family and colleagues get inspired. Sometimes they couldn't seem to get enough and they found the stories unbelievably motivating.

I love this story about how he and his best friend, during one of their capers, decided to apply for places in an all Girls' college because it was the only free school around them for miles.

Given the fact that dad had no one to pay his school fees, you can understand the desperation that led to the audacious and extremely unusual request, which the head teacher of an all Girls' school received from two young men who at this stage – I must add – were old enough to cause the girls and the school a lot of grief.

In their pursuit of college education, they realised they could not afford the tuition fees, uniforms, books, accommodation and everything else, even after years of saving up everything they had earned.

One night as they sat and tried to figure a way out, they thought of writing to all of the schools within their local area, requesting special grants to enable them to study.

They came up with all manner of skills they could barter for a place in one of the schools. Options ranged from working for their places within the school canteen, or any other areas, to being allowed to go home on the weekends to work and earn some money in time for Monday morning.

The boldest request however was made to a school that had a 'no boys' policy. Knowing this did not deter my dad and his friend from writing to the head teacher.

I'm sure they offered to sit at the back of the class, or do whatever it took to stay separate from the girls, but the head teacher, understandably but unfortunately, could not take them up on any of their offers.

My dad's relentless pursuit of an education would then lead him to take a job as a cook at a missionary school, just because it gave him the opportunity to stand in the corridor and learn through the classroom windows. He often told us he would write down notes from lessons on the blackboard before he cleaned the classrooms. He was glad when a teacher could not be bothered to wipe down the board as he got a chance to learn – if the blackboard was cleaned before he got into the classroom; he often wondered what he had missed.

This job also gave him access to the school library, which meant that he could study for free at nights, when everyone was in bed. This was how he not only saved up, but also learned for free. Eventually he got to a level where he could sit the relevant exams – which he passed – this enabled him to move on to higher education.

My father ultimately did his Bachelor of Arts degree in History and Geography after my brother and I were born. It took that long for him to finally achieve his dream of a University education, but he did. I was about five years old when he was doing his degree and my mum worked to support him and the family.

Many years later, I put this bold approach to life into practice when I applied for a job that was at least three levels above my grade at the time. I knew I could do the job and was qualified for it but, more importantly, I desperately wanted the promotion. I reminded myself, that if daddy could apply to an all Girls' school then I could go for this leap.

What's the worst thing that could happen?

The recruiting manager reminded me that this job was far higher than my current one but was happy for me to put in an application, which I did. My mentor at work and my colleagues also warned me that I was not meant to go for promotions within the first two years of being in a role.

Despite all of this, I went for it, passed the interview and got the job. Initially it was on a seconded basis but the promotion was made permanent four months later, almost doubling my annual income. It would have taken me, on average, four promotions (one every couple of years) to achieve this pay rise if I had not been bold enough to go after something that I really wanted.

My bold and audacious move accelerated my career by eight years. Thanks to my father's fearless attitude to life, I dare to dream and, more importantly, I dare to pursue those dreams relentlessly.

It is good to learn what to avoid by studying the misfortunes of others.

Publius Syrius

I learn gossip never pays – don't say behind people's backs what you are not prepared to say to their faces.

My father always enjoyed telling me this story about a family friend from his village. This man was known to be quite liberal and forward thinking, which was – and still is – a desirable quality.

Growing up in Nigeria, with its many languages, means that it is culturally easier to marry within your own tribe. Many tribes have different customs, ranging from how you behave around elders to how you relate to your in-laws. At its most extreme, the Yoruba culture would not allow a newly married wife to call any child, born into the extended family before the marriage date, by name. As far as they were concerned, the child was older than the woman in terms of the day they both joined the extended family and, therefore, was of a higher standing.

This often made for hilarious situations, as the wife would need to come up with an acceptable way to address the youngster, which would satisfy the elders' wish for her to respect the child as her superior but, at the same time, would allow her to still feel like a human being. Growing up, I could never understand this mentality but some people truly lived it.

Other cultures in Nigeria, spoke a language that did not enable the articulation of respect, as it was defined, pretty much like the English language. Those cultures tended to call everyone by their first names regardless of age. This was a big taboo in my culture given that my language, Yoruba, is rich enough to have different words and phrases, which are used depending on age, prominence and position of the person you are speaking to.

To use the wrong greeting or phrase would be seen as disrespectful to an older person and would be punishable by any adult who may be around at the time of the offence. It was not uncommon to be told off by a total stranger in the market place, that is why it is often said that it takes a village to raise a child.

Closely aligned to this, is the expectation that girls should curtsey for anyone older than themselves and, in some cases, your knees were expected to touch the ground especially for authority figures like parents, relatives and others in traditional chieftaincy positions. Some would even demand that you stay on your knees while addressing them or if they were talking to you and occasionally, you were expected to serve food or drinks while on your knees. I personally found this de-humanising and demoralising even as a child.

As with any other thing that can be abused, in-laws in Yoruba land considered a curtsey from the new wife to everyone in the family, their God given right. Even other women who had married into that family before you, would now consider themselves as the 'senior wives' forgetting how they felt when faced with this treatment. They would see a common target to demand respect from and the new wife would sometimes feel like a lamb being led to the slaughter.

Having an understanding of these cultures often makes the first few years of any marriage easier to navigate and is especially useful in getting the in-laws on side.

Well, one of my dad's friends married from outside the village, which would have been seen as an affront, but to make matters worse, the wife, did not even speak the language or understand her husband's culture! It was not a surprise when the ugly head of the 'culture serpent' was raised soon after they were married.

Some relatives had come from the village to visit them but unfortunately the husband was out. In her own way, the wife welcomed them, gave them water and cold drinks to help them recover after their long journey through a tropical climate. She left them to prepare their meals but unbeknown to her, she had offended them by not kneeling down to greet them when they first arrived. The guests ate the meal and waited for her husband to come home.

Once he returned, she excused herself to allow them some privacy and, perhaps, because she had no way of taking part in the conversation given the language barrier. Had she stayed and shown interest in the conversation, it would have been considered disrespectful – after all, it was the adults of the family talking and she was essentially the baby of the family in standing. In those days children were seen and not heard and speaking out of turn was asking for trouble.

What the missus of the house did not realise was that the visitors had chosen to make their views on her behaviour clear to her husband, before they even got to the purpose of their visit. My dad's friend listened to them and after they had aired their grievances, he asked his wife to come downstairs.

Readying themselves for an apology, the in-laws shifted themselves into more comfortable positions on the settees. They were shocked when the husband told them to repeat their complaints, with his wife present. This led to awkward glances and shuffling around with the relatives no longer comfortable.

There was no response from the settees and the man proceeded to tell them never to come into his home and criticise his wife or say behind her back what they were unwilling to say to her face. He taught them a lesson that went beyond culture 101, showing the best way – in my opinion – to deal with gossip and back stabbing.

My father said that on that day, the wife also resolved never to have any guests from the village in the main house, banishing them instead to a guest apartment within the grounds.

A lesson was learned that day and a village's attitude was changed when these people went back home and the news of the ordeal they had suffered spread through the entire village. People were told never to visit the couple unless they wanted to be insulted by the wife and her husband. Decent people from the village agreed behind closed doors that the man had done well and right by his wife, by refusing to allow his family to disrespect her. Others argued that he should have forced his wife to treat his family in the 'right and proper' way.

There were two versions of the story and two schools of thought depending on who you spoke to in the village. One believed that this man had been 'castrated' by his wife, making him subservient to her and causing him to rate her higher than his family. In the local parlance it would have been said that she had put his head under and in between her legs – this meant that she was in control of her husband and had him under her thumb.

The other school of thought – the one that my father and I subscribed to – saw the incident as a lesson in putting the in-laws in their place and, hopefully, the start of a culture shift where the husbands would see it as their duty to protect their wives from archaic cultures and people that would seek to abuse their imagined, and often deluded, "powers".

My father relished telling this particular tale because it resonated with him having grown up in the village. Also, his best friend, from all those years ago, ended up marrying someone from a similar village as the woman in the story and ended up having similar challenges.

For me, the main lesson I took away from this incident was never to say behind a person's back, what I am not prepared to say to their face.

There are people who put their dreams in a little box and say, Yes, I've got dreams, of course I've got dreams. Then they put the box away and bring it out once in awhile to look in it, and yep, they're still there.

Bombeck, Erna

I learn I can dare to have dreams because I have more chance of achieving them.

A day that I remember with great emotion was my first time in an airplane. I must have been about eight years old when daddy took my brother and I to a military base in northern Nigeria. We had an uncle who worked there and daddy arranged for us to visit him and get a guided tour of the base.

The highlight of the day was sitting in the cockpit of an aircraft. I felt on top of the world. I don't believe we took to the air but I recall feeling as though I was on my way to space.

It was an amazing and really special experience. When we came out of the plane, daddy told us that it could become our mode of transportation if we worked hard.

For a very young girl, a seed was planted, that someday I would be flying the skies. Looking back, it was a military helicopter that felt like a Boeing 747, but most importantly, the experience was enough for me to catch the vision and dare to dream big.

I always remember this trip anytime I am flying around the world; as I sink into my seat and fasten my seatbelt, I hear that voice inside my head telling me daddy was right. I am flying.

All our dreams can come true – if we have the courage to pursue them.

Disney, Walt

I learn no dream is too big or too far-fetched. It may take years and thousands of attempts, but if you can dream it, there will always be a way to make it happen. You just start and never give up until the dream is a reality.

Another vision that daddy introduced into our worlds was that of going on to further our education. I was still in junior school when daddy took my brother and I to a university campus. We sat down on the lush grass and watched the students go by.

To a young girl, this was the ultimate life. I saw young men and women strolling with their books, no parents in sight, and dressed in shabby chic fashion. I saw young lovers walking hand in hand with the guys hanging on the girls' every word.

I was hooked and could not wait to experience such freedom.

After a while, taking in the sights of the University grounds, daddy took us to a newly constructed lecture theatre. He went to the front while we sat and watched him pretend to be a lecturer. We took turns pretending to be students and lecturers. Daddy later came round and told us that someday, if we worked hard, we would be receiving lectures in that very hall someday.

This was a picture that stayed with me for many years and I still inspire people as I share this story with friends and colleagues.

It would take many years before I realised that my father was using a powerful tool of envisioning, broadening our minds, to create a picture of a future reality and help us to create powerful pictures in our minds that we could work towards.

Happy are those who dream dreams and are ready to pay the price to make them come true.

Leon J. Suenes

I learn every day is an opportunity for a lesson.

Daddy enjoyed taking us to botanical gardens. He had a love for all things in nature and he spent time, sharing this pleasure and joy with us. With daddy, nothing was ever as it appeared, consequently while in the botanical gardens, we learnt about plants, insects, rocks and all living things.

Life was always an adventure and an education. To our innocent minds, we were taking a break, but to my father, we were now on the practical side of learning.

As an educator he constantly found ways to impart knowledge and continually shared his experiences with us. Boy did he have a lot of life lessons to share! He had a dream for us and wove it into the fabric of our lives and our days. Everything he did was linked directly to making the dream a reality.

He loved to take us to the nicest part of the towns and cities, as he wanted to show us where we could live and the kinds of lives we could have. He never limited us to our current realities; rather, he kept on challenging our current realities with future possibilities.

He made us dream big and we grew up believing that anything is truly possible if we are willing to pursue it with dogged determination.

The people who get on in this world are the people who get up and look for the circumstances they want and if they can't find them, make them.

Shaw, George Bernard

I learn you must have a goal even though it can come with a risk of losing friends along the way.

Daddy always made sure we knew that we were his priorities. He spent all of his available time outside of work with his family and especially his children.

I recall that from the ages of six to ten, before I went to boarding school, we spent our evenings sat on a leather carpet and he would tell us story after story. He would share riddles and make us come up with the answers and it took a really long time before we realised that he made up some of the tales as he went along. We caught him out when he tried to retell a story and couldn't remember how it went.

I learnt to tell stories from him and he helped us to develop a powerful imagination, which has come in handy to this day. One of the most effortless things for me to do is to write or tell a story and my love for this art form came purely from having a father who devoted his time to us.

With every tale my father encouraged, challenged, inspired and occasionally scared us – but in a good way. There was always a lesson to be learned, good always trumped evil and hard work always paid off.

As I got older daddy stayed at home to coach us, help us study and even watch the television with us. We were his everything and he made sure that we not only knew this but also saw him demonstrate it every day.

His friends would show up and ask him to go out for a drink and, in most cases, daddy would say no. Even when he occasionally agreed to a drink, he would not hesitate to give us his full attention if we showed up with a book or a request.

His friends could not fathom how he could be so satisfied with his family and not seek much else but daddy was trying his very best to enjoy a blessing he never truly had as a child – the blessing of a family to call his very own; a family that loved him back and accepted him for who he was.

You had to know where he was coming from to understand his passion for his family.

I learnt from my father, that you must let those you love know they are important through any means possible; use your words, use your actions, use your time. Let your very existence tell the same story.

Whenever daddy was expecting one of us to come home, he would stroll to the main road a dozen times with eager anticipation, always looking out for our car and peering into every taxi window. He could not and would not stay still until we got home. We got used to this as well, expecting to see him along the road and we were actually disappointed if he was not there waiting. For me it was the first reminder of having been missed and feeling loved.

Ultimately he would give us his undivided attention as he caught up on all our news and within minutes, he would be bragging about us to anyone that cared to listen.

He knew how to make us feel wanted and adored. He did not have a lot of money but he had love and passion for his children and I would not trade that for all the money in the world.

We were everything to him.

Why be something to everybody when you can be everything to somebody?

Chesterton, GK

The power of imagination makes us infinite.

John Muir

I learn it is important to create memories that outlive you.

For me these memories were all about story time, passing gas, plaiting hair, chasing him round the house, mucking around and laughing together. Some of my greatest memories of my father were those where we were just having fun and being downright rude.

I recall daddy would ask us to get fluff off his pants and as I moved to do that, he would pass pretend gas (and occasionally real gas), I would screech, 'daddy!!!!!' and chase him round the house with the clear intent of smacking his bottom.

After a while he would let me catch him and give him the well deserved smack on the bottom and let out another fart sound, timing it to perfection.

We had loads of fun and laughed a lot. He never ceased to entertain us and he had a way with words as only a storyteller has.

I learnt to plait hair twiddling with his, as he sat patiently. I remember pushing his head round if he dared to move. I was this young girl who was intent on figuring out the plaits and he sat there, I guess in discomfort, never complaining, often getting a mirror and complimenting my work.

The memories he created have outlived him and are being passed on to the next generation, as we share the stories of their grand father.

People will always remember how you made them feel. As a father, he made us feel really special and worth it.

Be a family.

Have a laugh, be at your best, be at your worst sometimes, but know always that you are loved unconditionally and supported unwaveringly.

All experience is an arch to build upon.

Henry Brook Adams

I learn the truth about respect and understanding the difference between needs and wants.

My earliest experiences about money were at the age of seven, when my father told us about his income. He explained about earning a salary and paying for the fixed expenses including house rent, utility bills and giving my mum money for the groceries.

He told us that what was left was put inside a folder that contained his car documents. He always made a special effort to get brand new notes for the folder.

My brother and I were told we could help ourselves to the money if we needed to buy anything. Daddy made it clear that the money was the family's to spend but that when it was gone, it was gone.

I reckon a lot of people would assume that this was a mistake and that we were careless but they would be wrong. With that level of freedom came choice, empowerment, accountability and responsibility.

We would occasionally take some money but not without counting and checking that there was enough left.

Over time we learnt to first count what was left, work out the number of days till the next pay day and then we made our decision whether to take or not to take some of it.

I did not realise that I was learning accountability, budgeting and respect for other peoples' hard work, but that was exactly what we came to understand. We learnt that there is a difference between what we need and what we want and what we now know as delayed gratification.

We understood it was not appropriate to take advantage of other peoples' work and we learnt to respect not just my daddy but also his time – we were able to place non-monetary value on what he earned.

Daddy's folder was never empty and I never once saw him monitor the money or think that we would make the wrong decision and overspend. It was a mutually respectful relationship; as he trusted us, we rewarded him by being considerate.

New opinions are always suspected, and usually opposed, without any other reason but because they are not already common.

Locke, John

I learn not to disregard ideas; they might just hold the key to so much more.

Daddy was a visionary and wherever he looked, he saw possibilities. Growing up, my mum sold bottled water and I recall a day my father said it would be nice to flavour the water with lime, lemon, orange or any other seasonal fruit.

We all took this with a pinch of salt and my mum joked, making a comment about who would be bothered to buy water with a flavour.

Daddy must have mentioned this a number of times before giving up on the idea. For him it was just a suggestion as he was not entrepreneurial although he often had really great thoughts on how to grow the family business.

He constantly thought about forward and backward integration but my mum was content with the size of her business so she never really took a lot of his advice on board.

Almost two decades after my dad talked about flavoured water, I began to see it in supermarkets around the world and I can't but wonder what might have been if we had embraced his ideas way back in the eighties. Perhaps flavoured water was already a known product in other countries but in Nigeria, this would have been a truly novel concept, which could have made us really wealthy.

From this experience, I have learnt not to take any ideas for granted. What once seemed far fetched is now a staple product in people's weekly shopping and I wonder what my father would have thought or said if he was still alive.

He was a visionary and to this day, as a business improvement expert, I am always thinking of the grandest and most creative solutions to problems. All I see are possibilities and better ways to do things.

I learnt from my father that there are truly no limits in life. Dream it to achieve it. "Dare to dream" has become a core idea that I subscribe to.

Pick up a grain a day and add to your heap. You will soon learn, by happy experience, the power of littles as applied to intellectual processes and gains.

John S Hart

I learn the power of words through 'a book a week' – all and sundry and the joys of discovering new words.

As a young girl, I loved literature because my father inspired and helped me to cultivate a lifelong habit of reading. I read several books a week and when I was in secondary school, I often had a novel tucked in between my textbooks. To the outside world I was studying but I was actually lost in the magical world described in the books.

When I went to boarding school at the age of ten, daddy made me commit to reading a book a week and I had to write a letter once I had finished it, summarising the story and using some new words and phrases I had learnt.

I recall reading a book and coming across the phrase "all and sundry" which means 'everyone'. I could not wait to use the phrase and it was such a pleasure to write my letter, proudly finishing it with "all and sundry' send their love'. I was chuffed to bits and waited impatiently for his reply where he would quiz me on the new words and compliment me for a job well done.

As a father, he found a way to continue to stay in touch with my education and learning process even though I was miles away in a boarding school and only saw him once a month. We shared this passion for reading and he continued to nurture it albeit from afar.

He taught me that where there is a will, there is always a way and we can all make an effort to keep in touch, share a passion – perhaps a dream – but most importantly inspire someone to greatness.

A moment's insight is sometimes worth a life's experience.

Oliver Wendell Holmes

I learn that just because everyone is doing it doesn't mean it's for you – social drinking.

My brother and I learnt quite early on in life that you shouldn't follow the crowd and that just because something is a popular opinion does not mean you should agree with it. Dad lived this principle and it always came across in discussions with his friends, families and colleagues.

We would listen and watch him hold his own even when it was obvious that others did not agree with him. Occasionally I would think to myself that it would be easier to go with the flow, especially if someone was purposefully being obnoxious, but daddy always found it easy to make the person see the errors of their ways.

The one thing that truly reminds me of this was his approach to drinking. He was never a big drinker and even though we had the odd bottle of Schnapps and Dubonnet wine at home, he only ever had just a little at a time. He would occasionally let us try it, which was great as it meant that alcohol had no intrigue for me growing up. This came in handy as I never became overly drunk or got into the habit of drinking.

Well back to dad's drinking, or the lack of it. He was exclusively a social drinker and he would take his time over a glass of beer even with his friends. They would get through half a dozen glasses before my father would finish half of his first one.

We often wondered how he kept this going as his friends ribbed and riled him trying to get him to drink faster to keep up with their pace.

In their ploy to get him to drink more, they would order him fresh drinks which just sat on the table and were often either finished by his friends or cleared away by the bar staff.

I remember quite clearly the day he decided to stop completely. He said that, given that he never enjoyed drinking, he would stop entirely with no exceptions.

When his friends came round, as they often did, my father would order a round of drinks for them and none for himself. They all tried to get him to join in but he continued to say no.

We kept observing him day after day; the days turned into weeks and weeks into months, which soon turned into years and none of his friends got him to drink in all that time.

I was quite impressed as I saw him hold out as friend after friend failed in their attempt to get him to drink. Some of them would threaten not to have anything themselves and he would merely shrug his shoulders. These were empty threats as his friends continued to drink even when they could not get him to join them.

It soon became the new norm for them and we all got used to the new daddy – the complete non-drinker. Most importantly, I learnt to stand up for my beliefs and decisions even if they went against the grain and the expectations of others.

If we do not plant knowledge when young, it will give us no shade when we are old.

Lord Chesterfield

I learn that asking for help is a sign of strength, not one of weakness.

This was a huge lesson for me – one that I needed and one that would come in handy for many years to come.

We were at the farm and we needed to remove weeds from a portion of the land, which was set out in rows. My dad, my brother and I all had individual rows and I was struggling to weed mine. I tried my best to keep up with them because it never occurred to me that I was younger than them and less experienced than they were. I never knew that I was not meant to keep up with them; I just assumed that we all needed to keep the same pace doing what we were doing. Eventually I got really tired and, rather than stop to rest I kept up, but began to cry.

Soon enough my brother noticed I was crying and pointed it out to my father who was shocked that I was upset. He promptly asked me what had happened and I told him that I was tired and could not continue to weed at the same pace.

I was surprised at his response when he said that all I needed to do was stop and take a break. He went on to talk to my brother and I, telling us that whilst it is admirable to work hard, we need to know that it is okay to ask for help and to ask for it at the right time.

I learnt a really valuable lesson that day. I still demand excellence from myself and occasionally say 'yes' to too much but, now and again, I remind myself that it's okay to say 'no', it's okay to say 'I'm too tired', it's okay to admit I need help and sometimes it's even okay to walk away.

What progress, you ask, have I made? I have begun to be a friend to myself.

Hecato, Greek philosopher

I learn it is important to laugh even if it is at yourself.

I can't remember this story in great detail but the one thing I know was that dad was a bit of a joker. He never ceased to laugh, fool around and make others laugh. I reckon if he had been born in this generation, he would have been a stand up comedian.

He was not afraid to laugh at himself and have others laugh with him and sometimes at him. He seemed to thrive on making others smile. He was the kind of father who allowed me to put make-up on him, dress him up, plait his hair and then show the final work to everyone on the street.

Sometimes, I tied a head wrap on his head and made him wear my mum's shoes and clothes and he never once shied from showing off the result. There were the odd occasions when people would walk into my mum's room not realising my dad was sat on the chair looking gloriously different from usual.

This prompted my mum to tell us a story about how my father once dressed up as a woman (head gear, shoes and all) and even she did not recognise him when she came home, even though he was dressed in her clothes, just to get a laugh and a reaction from her.

She never ceased to laugh whenever she told this story, which was often, especially after my dad passed away.

For me I learnt that life was more fun when a lot of laughter is thrown in for and on the journey.

He who has never learned to obey cannot be a good commander.

Aristotle

I learn to follow instructions; they are there for a purpose.

I will never forget one particular day. It started like any other day but later in the afternoon my mum and dad asked us to go and get a haircut at the barbing salon.

There were four of us including two young relatives who were living with us. We took the money and were given express instructions to go to a specific barber whom we had always used and whose shop was reasonably close to the house.

On the way, someone had a brain wave – or so we thought – suggesting that we go to another barbing salon on the other side of town. To our minds, it sounded more like an adventure, which would allow us to be independent and be away from home for longer.

Being children, we must have misjudged how far the salon was. We walked there, got our haircuts and walked back. Considering we were chatting every step of the way and that we chose to go the longer route, we didn't realise just how long we had been away. I remember the sun had gone down before we got back and in a tropical climate that meant that it would have been at least 7pm.

At home, our parents were beside themselves with worry wondering how they would explain four children going missing in one day. Several search parties had gone out looking for us and some of them had returned with no success.

We were completely oblivious of what was going on or how long we had been away and we were shocked when we saw a lot of people at our house, wondering why they were all there. There was no end to the people who scolded us in true Nigerian fashion, reinforcing the belief that it takes a village to raise a child. Everyone asked why we would take so long and worry our parents.

Although we were only little, we knew that all hell had broken loose and that we were in for a talking to. We soon realised it was more serious when we saw the look on our parent's faces and it was evident that we were going to get a right good smack along the way. I recall that we were smacked according to age, starting with the oldest one amongst us.

I was not really good at dealing with being told off and as I waited my turn, it felt like eternity. I can honestly say that I felt each smack that my siblings were dealt like it had been applied to my behind while I was in the queue, waiting my turn.

By the time it came, I was shivering and sweaty at the same time and I felt sheer terror as I fumbled my way forward. I remember getting one smack, screaming really loudly and running to my grand mother, who promptly begged my father for mercy.

Thank God, he obliged and I got away with just one slap on the backside.

We were thoroughly told off and were sent straight to bed. I will never forget this day and I recall we all got the same treatment – although I got away lightly thanks to grandma coming to my rescue.

My father did not like violence but he felt on the odd occasion, an appropriate smack was needed to get the message home through our stubbornness. We often saw the regret on his face whenever he resorted to a smack rather than just a stern look or words.

You gain strength, experience and confidence by every experience where you really stop to look fear in the face. You must do the thing you cannot do.

Roosevelt, Eleanor

I learn when it comes to some things, once is too many.

We grew up knowing that violence was not allowed in our home, but we took this lesson to school as well and I look back over my life knowing that I never had a physical fight with another student.

My dad took this lesson further when we began to date. He linked it to a need for us girls to take our education seriously as, in his opinion, the worst situation a woman could be in would be one where she felt that she had no choice in a relationship because she could not provide for herself.

He always reminded me that when you feel you have no choice, you stay in a mess longer than you should. For him the mess could be a bad relationship or a bad marriage but, worst of all, was a marriage where physical abuse was happening.

He often said once is too many when it comes to domestic abuse. As much as he believed in forgiveness, this was the one offence for which no apology would be acceptable. He had seen too many weak, fake and ill-informed apologies and he had seen way too many broken promises.

He made us realise our worth and often said he had seen many battered women stay in those relationships because they had no other means of caring for their children and themselves.

He told us it would be hard but realistic for a woman to leave the physically abusive relationship if they felt they had an understanding home and family to go back to or if they at least had an education or a career to fall back on.

To reiterate this lesson, he told us a story about when he married our mum. He told her at the start of the relationship that he did not believe in violence in general and was strongly against violence in the home.

He told her his plan for if he ever felt provoked enough to be physically abusive. The plan was that he would suggest that she visit her family and he would send her home with a letter to her father. He described the content of the letter to us vividly and we would laugh picturing my grandfather's face if he got a note asking him to kindly keep his daughter at home because her husband was finding it hard to resist hitting her.

We laughed but the lesson was very clear to us. We deserve better than that and, for the boys among us, no one, absolutely no one deserves to be hit no matter what.

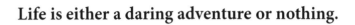

Life is either a daring adventure or nothing.

Helen Keller

I learn the importance of fighting back when the occasion warrants it – 'Come out from under the bed, you coward'.

One of the options, if you are in an abusive relationship or if you are being bullied, is to fight back and one woman did this when we were growing up.

When this happened, as children, we were excited with the buzz in the atmosphere and the intense drama of the situation so we tried to catch a glimpse of it all. There were adults who shooed us away so we could not wait for my dad to come home and fill in the gaps.

The woman had often been verbally abused by her husband and, in a lot of cases, even physically. She would cry out and the elders in the community would go and try to resolve the conflict.

My parents often had to get involved but my dad especially hated it, often commenting that something had to change if the woman was to have a decent life.

One day something did change or more precisely, something seemed to snap in the woman and she chose to fight back. She screamed at her husband and came at him like a wild bulldog having a psychotic episode.

I'm not sure whether it was the shock of seeing his wife in this state or the fear that he had finally pushed her over the edge, but whatever it was turned the man into jelly and he fled.

The man ran across the road to a neighbour's house with his wife charging after him with a big stick, threatening that one of them would die that day and that she would be damned if the corpse was hers. People came to the door to try to stop the woman from entering the house but she managed to get in at which point she found her husband under the bed and promptly dragged him out by his shirt collar.

She did not quite get the satisfaction of hitting him as us kids hoped, but she managed to scare the living daylights out of him, making it quite clear that if he so much as raised his voice or hand to her again, it would be the last time he would have been able to use either of them.

I loved that day; it was truly one of the most liberating days of my life.

My dad simply said, "good for her. She got her freedom today".

If your actions inspire others to dream more, do more and become more, you are a leader.

John Quincy Adams

I learn I am good enough.

I was home schooled till I was six years old and then my dad decided it was time to go to a formal school. I remember standing in the head mistress's office, watching as they talked about me.

She wanted to know what year to place me in and sought my dad's view on what I could or could not do. My dad looked around her office and saw a dictionary, a Bible and some other books. He told her to select any book and have me read it.

She looked a bit sceptical as these were not children's books by any standard but my dad remained unconcerned. She handed me a Bible, which I opened up and began to read, much to her amazement.

Then she handed me the Oxford English Dictionary from which I also read fluently. She proceeded to test my knowledge of the 'multiplication tables' and again I passed with flying colours, starting with year 1 and moving right through to the year 3 books.

She was really impressed and decided I was too intelligent to start in nursery or year 1 but that I was too young to go into year 3, even though I could do everything that children at that level were expected to. That settled the decision on year 2.

As we walked out of the office, my father looked at me and said, "I told you, you are good enough"

I guess I must have had some apprehension but that comment laid all of them to rest. I soon started school and ended up doing my leaving exams when I was in year 5. I can still remember scrambling from the year 5 exams to year 6 to do their papers as well.

I was successful in both sets and ended up getting into secondary school when I was just ten. This taught me some useful lessons including the fact that I did not have to go with the flow in life. It was unusual to skip school years at the time but it happened.

The object of teaching a child is to enable him to get along without a teacher.

Hubbard, Elbert

I learn that every lesson will get an opportunity to be tested – 'I leave school at the age of ten and have to stand up for myself, all because I had been raised not to run away from a fight just because I was scared'.

I had been accepted into a top boarding school where my classmates were children of the crème de la crème of society – the power brokers, politicians, and businessmen.

There were children of former presidents, current president and governors; some of these children had their own security detail and people that carried their luggage to the boarding house. These kids spent all their summers abroad and had no clue what a chore was.

I remember there was this girl who realised she would have to wash her own clothes. There were no washing machines or maids to clean up after her. She thought washing her own panties was the filthiest act imaginable. She decided that she couldn't or wouldn't wash them.

Each day, she threw away her used pants and this went on for almost a month until she realised that there was only one pair left. It was like watching a reality TV show as everyone waited with baited breath to see whether these pants would also be thrown in the bin. The only choices left were to wash them or go commando.

We all watched as she eowwed and aaarghed her way through washing her panties. It was a sight to see. She had to towel dry them and hang them by a ceiling fan to dry before they were ready to wear.

There was always a drama of some sort as these people, who for the most part felt entitled and had no appreciation for hard work, lived their lives amongst the mere mortals such as me.

Before I left home, my father had reminded me never to forget who I was on the inside, never to stop believing in myself and finally to remember whose daughter I was. I was only ten and petrified but held on to those words.

The one thing I took away from his pep talk was that I had to be fearless and strong because I was on my own with no one around me.

I was the sort of person who saw everything in black and white, with no shades of grey in between; I either liked you or didn't, if I was angry with you, you would know. I did not know how to pretend and I took peoples' words literally.

As part of induction, we were told the school rules and regulations that included no fagging, no bullying and that everyone was responsible for their own chores. I was sold on it all.

A few weeks into the school year, there was this really tall senior student who asked me to wash her bed sheets, to which I said no. For me this was an easy decision – after all, everyone was responsible for his or her own chores. Simple!!! Right? Apparently not!

I politely declined to wash the clothes and she got upset. How dare I, who was I to decline? She had friends who were egging her on and she felt entitled as a senior student but I simply felt that I was obeying the school rules by saying no.

She threatened me and put her dirty clothes on my bed and I in turn promptly took them back to her room. This continued over a couple of days as we approached the weekly Saturday inspection from the school Principal and housemistresses. These were tough days, starting very early, at six in the morning, and we all wanted to come first in the battle of 'the houses'.

About thirty minutes before the inspection, the girl came and took my clean sheets off my bed and threw hers on my mattress. Everyone watched for what I would do. She was twice my size, looked like an Amazon and dragon all wrapped in one. As my parents were not wealthy, I did not have the luxury of loads of sheets so I just waited.

There was no way I was going to be cheated by another human being. As the inspections began in her room, I walked in through the opposite adjoining doors and yanked my sheets off her bed and replaced them with her dirty sheets just as the School Principal looked up and saw what was going on.

Her room failed the inspection on that account and I was still trying to make my bed as the Headmistress and her colleagues got to my room. Obviously they knew something was going on and they stopped in front of my bed to question me. I responded honestly and told them I was simply abiding by what I was told. My voice was shaky as I was close to tears but I managed to hold myself together through it all.

The girl was told off and asked to sweep her dormitory as punishment. When she had finished, she came to my room and told me to sweep four rooms for my punishment. Off I went to the school Principal's house to report this turn of events. I was told not to sweep the rooms but as her punishment she was now asked to sweep sixteen rooms.

We seemed to be doing a dance, she attempting to punish me, me running to the School Principal (who at this time knew me by name) and in turn increasing her punishment.

I don't know what really happened but the more I stood my ground, the more she seemed to run out of steam, eventually giving up on me altogether. I never again had an encounter with her. We walked past one another along the corridors without acknowledging each other's existence over the next few years.

I was only ten and found myself confronting a fifteen-year-old senior. This experience would come in handy in future conflicts which I also overcame by standing up for what was right and more importantly standing up for myself.

We need men who can dream of things that never were.

Kennedy, John F

I learn it is important to feed a child's dream because you never know where it will end.

I was only seven years old when my father encouraged me to write some stories. As a family we had story telling every evening and my father made up a lot of far-fetched ones so it was easy to let my imaginations run riot.

I remembered writing my first story, which my father took to his office and had his secretary type it up. Seeing my manuscript was the most amazing feeling that I had ever had. A few days later, my dad gave me a paper back bound book and it had my name on the front page as the author.

Looking back, it was simply bound – nothing fancy – but it made me feel like the most important person in the world. I soon wrote more stories that my dad also collected into a book.

A love of writing was born simply because my dad planted the seed first by telling stories and helping me to dream, then by turning my dreams into my first two books.

This love continues to this day and led to what you're reading today and I can't thank him enough.

Life is like a game of cards. The hand that is dealt you represents determinism; the way you play it is free will.

Jawaharal Nehru

I learn about the gift of forgiveness – it's something you give yourself first and others second because you end up gaining so much more than you ever have to give.

As a child, I remember that my father was more than capable of holding a grudge. For example, he could make the entire summer holiday hell if we brought home an average report. Day after day, night after night, he would be tough on us and he would keep this going, giving the impression that he would never be able to forgive the incident.

Despite this, when I consider his relationship with his mother, I can't but see him as the most forgiving person I know. To understand this, you will need to know how he grew up.

In today's world, it would be said that he grew up in a dysfunctional family and nowadays he would have been in therapy his whole life, just to help him function. When my father told us his stories, I could not but feel his pain.

My grand mother fell out with her husband and they went their separate ways but during this separation, she began to date someone else. In our culture in those days, separation and divorce were unheard of and completely unacceptable. Her parents would not hear anything of it and she was soon forced to go back to her husband, which she did.

As if life could not get any more complicated, she soon found out that she was pregnant with her boyfriend's baby. This was another taboo and decisions were made that meant she stayed with her husband rather than go back to the father of her baby. The family assumed that her husband would eventually forgive and forget but I guess it was not that easy for him to do. After my dad was born, his mum had to juggle pleasing her husband with raising a child who, in the true sense of the word, was not his.

It soon became obvious that she chose her husband over her

child's well being and, as my dad would recount later, he had to fend for himself from a very young age. He never even knew where his next meal would come from.

His step father did not accept him and his biological father also decided to stay out of his life, perhaps in a bid to punish his mum for going back to her husband or just to avoid dealing with the complication and the mess. My father often said he might as well have been an orphan even though there were three adults who could have chosen to love him and care for him, knowing full well that none of the mess was his fault.

No one did.

When he was old enough to start school, no one would pay for his school uniform or buy his books. His biological father was wealthy and paid for his other children to go to school but refused to pay for my father. Dad had no choice but to run errands for people in exchange for money, which he saved up. As he got older he began to go work for others on their farms for a wage, which he saved

This became his life.

He understood that his destiny was his to pursue on his own and he had no family to back him up. He had God and one friend.

From this humble beginning, my father worked all his life and saved enough to go to school, taking the long journey to eventually get his degree. Through all this time, my father saved enough to build a house for his mother and many years later when his biological father fell seriously ill, it was my dad, who came back to pay his medical bills and nursed him back to health.

Over the years, I have often wondered how my father could love his family – and keep on loving them – in spite of the fact that they struggled to love him back. If this was a one-off that would be easier to swallow, but growing up, I don't think I ever saw them truly change their attitude towards him. Time and time again, I felt angry on my father's behalf and, had I not been raised well, I would have let it rip on numerous occasions.

I remember the day my mum bought a mattress and insisted on taking it to the village. My father was not due to go back to the village for another month so the sense of urgency did not make any sense to me but mum bought it and had it delivered. I would later hear what had led to this seemingly urgent and irrational request.

My father, as a government worker, got paid at the end of each month and as soon as he received his salary, he would travel to the village to give his mum her allowance. This money paid for her medications, clothing and food and she even had enough to support her other sons who lived in the house with their families.

One would assume that my father's visit would be treasured and appreciated, as it was a key source of income. They appeared to merely see it as their payday and there was not much else to it.

On one of those infamous visits, my father gave his mum the money and other groceries he had bought for her as soon as he arrived in the evening. He went to his room to put his luggage down and decided to go and visit his friend. By the time he came back from his friend's house and got back to his room, he found that the mattress was no longer on the bed.

After playing detective with no luck, his mother told him that the mattress belonged to his younger brother and she had told him to go take it. The sad thing was that my uncle had disposed of my father's old mattress when he took over his room. He had his own rooms but had decided he needed more space and taking over his brother's only bedroom seemed to be an acceptable option to him forgetting that it was dad who actually built the house and paid for any repairs and maintenance.

In any culture, you would assume that the son that only comes round once a month will get the nice welcome, the choice cut of meat and if there was one bed that would be his. In our culture, there is naturally a lot of respect that is accorded to the first-born son, which my father was, but that did not seem to be the case for him.

Among his family, there was no regard for his position as the first-born son or that he only came round to visit once a month while his brothers lived at home and there was definitely no regard for the fact that the only reason he was home was to bring his mum money, which they all benefited from.

None of that mattered as his own mother told his younger brother to remove a mattress knowing fully well that her older son would have nothing but the metal springs on the bed to sleep on. My father had to flatten some cardboard boxes so there would be something between his body and the cold metal bed. There was no remorse from anyone; I guess they felt justified because the fact was that the owner of the mattress took it.

When my father got back home and told my mother what had happened, she burst into tears and made a decision that day that she would buy a new mattress and put a lock on the door of the only room in the house that my father used when he was visiting.

My mother did this and I was really proud but, as a young girl, my mind could not comprehend how or why a mother would treat one of her own children that way. The most amazing thing for me was that no matter what happened, my father never stopped going home or paying for his mum's upkeep.

To this moment, I don't know how he kept going or how he kept loving and definitely how he kept giving but I will always admire him for doing so.

He knew his own extended family did not love him unreservedly so his wife and children became his whole life and he looked to us for all the love he missed out on.

It was a heavy burden to bear as a child and to this day I still have unanswered questions.

Govern thy life and thoughts as if the whole world were to see the one, and read the other.

Thomas Fuller

I learn love is hard because sometimes it requires the pain of discipline.

As loving as my father was, he had his moments. In those moments I sometimes felt that he did not care enough; sometimes I even thought that he hated us.

He would lose his temper if we did not do the right thing but, more importantly, he would really be livid if we brought home 'bad' results – and by bad, I mean average. With my father, there was only one acceptable position and that was the top. Anything else was just not good enough.

I remember one year, I came home with the news that I came eleventh in the examination league table out of a class of thirty-one students. Bearing in mind that this was a secondary school where only children who had the best results from their primary education could gain admission, my results would easily have been the best in a lot of other schools.

This did not matter to my father, as all he saw was that I did not do well by his standards. Throughout that summer holiday, I felt like I was told off for every little offence and I could not catch a break. My father made me do so many chores that I had little time to rest: according to him, if I wanted to be lazy, then I needed to learn how hard life would be when the only career I would be suitable for would involve manual labour.

Life was tough and at moments, I felt some animosity towards him, as my mind could not comprehend why anyone would treat someone they loved so badly.

What I did not realise, was that he was using tough love as he did not want me to end up in a situation where I did not have much going for me. The only way he knew to make me work hard was to make life really difficult – so difficult that I would vow never to be in that position in the future.

Funny enough, after that experience, I did not always bring home the best results but I guess my father already knew I was doing my best or, perhaps, he was just tired of the tough love.

Deep down, I think he understood that I was the kind of person who tried not to make the same mistake twice and he also knew that he had put the fear of laziness and mediocre work into me for good.

People often say I am tough on myself and always have expectations that are way too high but I smile and think, I learnt from the best because I learnt from my father – a man who struggled most of his life but vowed that none of his children would suffer the same fate.

I have learnt to appreciate his toughness because I now know he was preparing me for a life that was worth living.

Educate your children to self-control, to the habit of holding passion and prejudice and evil tendencies subject to an upright and reasoning will, and you have done much to abolish misery from their future and crimes from society.

Franklin, Benjamin

I learn that violence is never the answer.

Growing up, there always seemed to be young relatives living with us, whether it was because their parents considered them a lost cause or just hoped that we would be able to provide better lives for their children.

The lost causes were often youngsters whose parents were at their wits' end, not knowing what to do about their truancy, disobedience, rudeness or persistent failure at school.

Some of these children came to us in unfortunate situations like the loss of a parent and, in one case, both parents within a relatively short period of time. Sometimes they came just for the holidays but occasionally for much longer periods. It all depended on the desperation of their parents.

Some parents left their child and never once checked on how he or she was faring but there were others who would visit once or twice a year.

When I was about seven, a family friend lost her husband and sent her eldest son to live with us as she was struggling to parent him while providing for the rest of the family. I guess the loss of his father sent him spinning and reeling, leaving him to lash out at his mum and siblings.

About the same time, my mum came home with a young girl who had lost both her parents. Her older siblings were too young to look after her and there were no relatives who could afford to take her in. She was a little bit older than the boy and they never stopped bickering.

One of the rules in our house was that we were not allowed to fight physically. We were expected to report any provocations or altercations to our parents who would resolve them and, more often than not, tell a story to help us understand the lesson that needed to be learnt.

This boy and girl never stopped quarrelling, which often resulted in some pushing, shoving and the occasional punch thrown in for good measure. I never quite understood why they constantly fought but I always called out to them if my father was coming. They would attempt a false truce just long enough for my dad to pass by at which point they would launch at each other again, picking up from where they left off.

There were the odd occasions when my dad witnessed the fight and he would sit them down for a lecture. In my young mind, this seemed to go on for years but I am sure it was more like weeks.

On one of those occasions, my father decided that he had had enough of the squabbles and that it was time to get the fight bug exorcised out of both of them. He saw them brawling and they stopped as soon as they noticed him but he told them to continue as they were.

Initially they were too stunned to carry on, wondering if they had heard him correctly. He asked one of us to get him a chair and the rest of us kids to sit down, pretty much simulating a boxing ring.

He proceeded to ask them to resume the fight, at which point they tried to tell him what had led to it in the first place. My dad told them that he was not interested in the lead-up; he just wanted to see them finish what they had started.

The fight resumed with reluctance from both parties but the gusto was missing and they soon fizzled out. Each time they attempted to stop, my dad would remind them that they needed to carry on given that this was what they truly wanted, otherwise they would not have resorted to this as a matter of course for conflict resolution.

This carried on for what seemed ages. They were both sweating and both were scratched and bruised because there were moments when they really got into the fight as one of them landed a really good punch. Eventually they stopped and told my dad they were tired.

After what seemed like an eternity they both crumpled to the floor absolutely shattered and my dad asked how that felt for them. He asked them to describe the pleasures and joys they derived from the fight, but neither of them had anything left to say.

He then proceeded to tell them there was no pleasure in fighting or inflicting pain on another person. He described how all conflicts could be resolved in non-physical ways and how one could always choose to walk away because fights would not happen unless there were two willing participants.

He reiterated the rules of his house and we were all reminded that not only was violence unacceptable in our home, it was not required in life.

Suffice it to say that was the last fight I witnessed in our house for a really long time. I guess we all learned that lesson real good but every few years, as new people came to live with us, the lesson was most likely refreshed for the benefits of the newbies until they also realised they had come into a 'no-fighting' home.

Life is like a library owned by the author. In it are a few books which he wrote himself, but most of them were written for him.

Harry Emerson Fosdick

I learn to help others 'get it 'and my love for coaching is born.

Ever since I was in primary school, my father encouraged me to help other children learn their schoolwork. When I look back now, I think the word 'encouraged' is being very generous as my father pretty much volunteered my tutoring services to anyone who needed them.

It was not unusual for me to spend the whole of my summer holiday coaching different students in all manners of subjects. Lots of people knew my father as a teacher so they would call on him any time their children brought home a bad school report. He in turn would offer my tuition to their children and he would inform me of who I would be helping that summer or in the evenings after each school day.

I always enjoyed the sessions. I would like to think that it is because I was giving back to those young boys and girls and it was probably partly to do with my ego being stroked but more than anything else, I enjoyed seeing them 'get it'.

For me it was a triumphant moment when I got my charges to understand something that had previously been beyond them.

I can remember looking for fun ways to get their heads around various topics. My father would often come round to check how we were getting on and my mum was on hand to provide lunch and snacks.

At the end of each day, after the students had left, my father and I would talk about their time with me. During this time I would talk about the topics they got wrong, the examples that helped them get it and the emotions of it all as some of them would be frustrated and sometimes threaten to give up or give in to the notion that they would never understand the topic.

My father would then give alternative views and approaches. Little did I know that my father was providing me with feedback that helped me to be a better coach.

Thirty years on, now I realise that, what my father was doing in continuous improvement and Lean terms, was process confirming me, doing Gemba activities and providing coaching and feedback enabling me to do a better job.

And boy, I am grateful today.

"An investment in knowledge pays the best interest."

Franklin, Benjamin

I learn it does not take much to make anyone feel special – 'my polka dot dress'.

One of the best days of my childhood was the day my father came back from a business trip with a dress for me.

The dress was made from soft jersey fabric and it had a white background with green, navy blue, purple and black polka dots. The sleeves were lined with green satin fabric and it had an elasticated waistband. It is still one of the best dresses I have ever had in my opinion.

It was all about how the dress made me feel – I felt really special and like I was worth a million dollars.

You would need to know a bit about my childhood to help you understand what the big deal was with the dress. Up until that day, my dad had only ever bought us books. There were no toys, no dresses, and no bicycles but there were always books, books and even more books. Ever since I could remember, encyclopedia Britannica and many other books, that were my body size and weight, surrounded me.

Clothes were more of a necessity during my childhood. My parents made enough money for us not to go hungry, they were able to cover all bills but we were not rich by any standard. Any money left over went on books and, in our house, books held their own against any other expenses. We were guaranteed new clothes at Easter, Christmas and New Year but my father brought home books almost on weekly basis.

So it was the surprise of the decade when my father came home with the "polka dot dress", I don't know what made him buy it, but I will always remember the way it made me feel.

In my mother's eyes, the dress confirmed her convictions that I was my father's favourite. That was the only time when my father bought me a dress instead of a book.

To this day, I have a soft spot for polka dots.

In life, a little surprise here and there should be thrown in. A little treat can go a long way, especially when it is a thoughtful one.

I love clothes now, but I love books just as much.

We make our fortunes, and we call them fate.

Earl of Beaconsfield

I learn being a parent is all about sacrifice – saving the best for your children.

I was not a great eater when I was young but I always loved meat. I could survive on Coca Cola and meat alone. My father knew this about me and he always left his meat for me.

In fact, I can't recall my father ever finishing his food if we were around. He would insist on us eating with him and leaving us some choice bits. Most times we would have eaten before he got home, but once my mum set his food in front of him, he would call us, ask if we were hungry and he was not too happy if we said 'no'.

My mum was not too impressed with him when he did this as she would have put the best cuts of meat for him and she knew it was more than likely that one of us children would end up with it. Looking back now she probably felt that we were depriving my father and her from those cuts of meat.

My father would insist on us eating with him and my mum would, in turn, insist that we had already had our dinners and we were not hungry. Daddy never enjoyed eating alone and it took a while for my mum to really understand how much it mattered to him that we shared his food.

Even when I told my dad that I was not hungry, so as not to offend my mum, my dad would sneak the meat, come over and sit next to me and would slide the meat onto my plate. More often than not, my mum caught him in the act as she had wised up to my dad, knowing the kind of person he was.

On a good day, my mum would be mildly annoyed but on a bad day, she would be really upset that my father was not eating – she saw his giving us the food from his plate as a waste because we weren't really hungry whereas he should have been.

I recall the day the message sank in for my mum. My father

had come home from work and insisted on us sharing his food when my mum said 'no'. He refused to eat and burst into tears asking my mum why she would not let his children share his food with him. He said that there was no joy or satisfaction if he could not share it with us. That was the last time my mum got involved in the discussions.

Occasionally she would mumble when dishing out his food that the food would end up in his children's stomachs anyway but she learned to keep her dissatisfaction to herself.

I recall a day that my father picked me up from the Boarding school I attended during visiting day and took me to the hotel he was staying at, called the White House Hotel. He ordered food as well as an extra plate of meat and he sat back watching me eat. He did not have that much himself and put as much as I could eat on my plate.

Another food experience I recall was a day that my father cried because I did not eat, as I should. At the time I lived on soft drinks and, as long as I had access to them, I could care less about food. I guess at a point my father must have been really concerned about the impact on my health but I did not think there was a problem. It was a shock to my system when he began to weep saying, 'how can someone not eat?"

Well, I began to eat and I have never stopped to this day. I wish he were here now as I could do with some reverse psychology – now I need to eat less.

The one lesson for me here was that he had his values, one of which was to put his children first and make sacrifices for them.

And he would not let any one stand in his way.

You cannot dream yourself into a character; you must hammer and forge yourself into one.

Henry David Thoreau

I learn the importance of honesty and integrity – 'If not for his honesty – we could have had everything. Or so I thought'.

My father was an idealist, he loved to talk politics with his friends and I loved to take part in those debates. I developed a desire to protect the vulnerable as a result of those discussions.

Bribery was rife when I was growing up in Nigeria and it got worse over the years. My father was in several key positions over his career and he was offered bribes on numerous occasions however he would always turn them down for the greater good. He lost friends because they had received bribes and turned a blind eye to unfinished building projects, which they had been paid for, such as school libraries.

My father could not comprehend why anyone would do that. I remember there was a time he was responsible for all the books that would be recommended to the State schools and consequently publishers would seek him out. I remember coming back from school one day and there was a TV or radio that had been dropped by one of the agents from a publishing company.

As a child I was really excited, obviously not aware of the source, about the free gift and we could not wait for my father to come back so we could all enjoy it. You can only imagine my shock and dismay when my father insisted on returning the gadget to the person who had brought it to his house. He would not touch it with a barge pole.

In my own little mind I thought – "if it is a gift, why can't we keep it?" When my father explained the reason for said gift, I could not help thinking that we could still keep it and make the right decision, which could mean that the giver would still not win the contract.

It would be many more years before I fully understood that it was not as black and white as I thought.

I am glad he set a great example for us, but over the years, I saw many people whose lives were different from ours simply because their fathers chose to accept and give bribes.

"Real integrity is doing the right thing, knowing that nobody's going to know whether you did it or not."

Winfrey, Oprah

I learn to pay attention to the needs of people around me rather than wait to be asked – 'I shouldn't have to ask and now an old dog can't learn new tricks ...'

Of all the lessons that my father left behind, this one is the one that I am not sure has been to my advantage and to this day I struggle with it.

Growing up with my dad taught me to have an expectation of people doing the right thing just because it is the right thing to do. I never needed to ask for anything from him because he seemed to know what I needed without me having to ask and he never kept anything back from us as children.

We knew where all his money was and we had free access to it. He told my brother and I to take whatever we needed whenever we needed it. We both knew that everything he had was in that one place and we were careful with his money as we never wanted to abuse the trust he had in us.

Over time I learnt to mask my needs or wants if I thought he could not afford it. I became a master of deception for want of a better phrase. I did not want him to feel bad that he could not provide for all the things I wanted, so it was easier to pretend that I did not want anything other than what he could afford to give me.

I buried a lot of desires deep down but more importantly I got used to never asking people to do things for me, I simply have an expectation that people will always do the right thing by me like my father did.

The very thought that I should have to tell someone to do the right thing means that I never truly appreciate what they do; it means more to me if they choose to do so themselves.

It also means that, over the years, a lot of people have offended me because they did not have my best interests at heart while others have endeared themselves to my heart because of the choices they have made and the things they have done for me without me having to ask.

There are some people who have earned a special place in my heart and life because they were exactly like my father in that I never needed to ask them for anything. They shared what they had with me, pre-empted and met the needs that I did not dare to articulate.

Lots of things that couldn't be done have been done.

Charles Auston Bates

I learn 'You can't rely on others to do your job for you'.

My father always worried about being there long enough to take care of his children and his wife. For a really long time, he tried to sponsor every member of my mum's family that he could lay his hands on. He wanted them to go to school, get decent jobs so they could have the ability to take care of themselves in the future.

There were times when I wondered why my father did not give up on people who did not appear to have the same desires for themselves as he had for them. One day he told my brother and I that he wanted my mum's siblings to do really well so that if he died too soon, they would be able to take care of their sister and us.

There is no welfare system in Nigeria, which means that, as people grow old, they only have their savings, any retirement benefits and their children as the sources of support. My father knew he had no savings, no houses to leave to his family and, because we were still so young, he opted for the next best thing which was to support his mum's family so that they could, in turn, support us if he was unable to do so.

It made sense on paper but it never quite worked out. None of those people who he thought would be there for us bought into his vision so eventually he had to hope that he could get as much of the job done as he could.

It was his prayer every day that he would live long enough for his children to be able to stand on their own two feet and have the ability to take care of his wife.

After my brother and I finished our first degrees and I got my Masters in Business Administration, my father began to relax and occasionally he would comment that if anything happened to him, he knew that my brother and I would take care of our siblings as well as our mum. I don't think he ever worried about dying after that day.

This made him very happy and one day he said, "I thank God that my children will be able to do what I thought I would have to rely on someone else to do for me" and we all knew exactly what he was talking about.

My father passed away before my younger siblings went to University but my brother and I made his dreams come true as we supported them through all their studies and took care of his wife.

I guess you could say he had his prayers answered and his soul can truly rest in peace.

The only way of finding the limits of the possible is by going beyond them into the impossible.

Arthur C. Clarke

I learn love compels – 'my science teaching history teacher'.

My father did a Bachelor of Arts in History and Geography so it was easy for him to help us in these two subjects.

What amazed me growing up was that he also taught us the entire science subjects although they were not his strong points. He would spend his evenings and weekends reviewing a chapter in a book or a subject from which he would create his own lesson plan and use that to teach us.

This just seemed to be the norm as we saw him poring over a Biology textbook and it took a number of years for us to realise that he had no choice but to first invest a few hours in those science subjects as that was the only way he could teach us. He had to learn it first, become a subject matter expert, and then teach us.

As my children have grown older, I have found myself downloading their school books and spending hours learning a subject just so that I can offer them the support they need in that subject.

It is easy for me to make a sacrifice because someone else has already made some for me. My father had given much of his time to me and set me a wonderful example that has helped me to see that anything I do for my children is merely continuing a legacy, that I hope will impact their lives positively.

Until you value yourself, you won't value your time. Until you value your time, you will not do anything with it.

M. Scott Peck

I learn it is important to know your self worth.

My father felt strongly about women knowing their self worth and I don't know where this point of view came from. My hypothesis would be that it had to do with his childhood.

He believed in women being empowered not in a *political* 'women's liberation' sort of way but in a *survival* 'women's liberation' way. He believed that women needed to have choices and that those choices defined your ability to take care of yourself.

He drummed it into me that if I had to look to somebody to meet all my needs, I had already given away all my power and ability to make choices to that person. Imagine if that person were physically, emotionally or verbally abusive, what would my options be? He thought that fear crippled too many people and, especially, kept women in situations they should not be in for longer than necessary.

He always told us that one of the most empowering things for a woman is to believe she has the potential to be somebody and to also have the capability to realise that potential. It was all about knowing you were capable of becoming whatever you wanted to be and pursuing whatever you set your heart to. For him the capability was all about being educated to the right standards and having the appropriate skills to achieve your goals. The final pieces in the jigsaw were not being afraid to make a choice and having a desire for perfection on your journey.

I say to people, if my dad were alive, I would have had my Doctorate degree by now. Stopping at a Masters degree level would not have been acceptable.

While he was not an advocate for divorce, he made it clear that he supported it over knowing that one of his daughters was in a situation where they felt powerless.

The other opinion my dad had on partnership was that one

should never date someone because of his or her wealth or social status. As far as he was concerned, when you say yes to any guy just because he has a decent income, you are indirectly acknowledging that you lack the ability, capacity and capability to earn that level of income yourself.

If you truly believed you had the same earning potential or could build the same company, then those factors would not be the deciding factors in who you date. He made me believe that I could be with a poor person and work with them to become as rich as we could imagine or as rich as we wanted to be.

With him there was no limit to what I could achieve which meant that I did not have to compare myself to others, I merely had to focus on me thereby freeing me to choose relationships purely based on non-material factors like love.

To this day, I don't know how to look to a man to supply material things or ask them for money.

If someone chooses to give me something, then I am appreciative but rather than ask, I think of a way to earn.

Talents are best nurtured in solitude, but character is best formed in the stormy billows of the world.

Johann Wolfgang von Goethe

I learn I have a choice and a voice.

I grew up amidst a number of tragedies. My mum had lost three children successively and our house became the place where there was always a concern for our safety.

My parents always tried everything in their power to protect us, and rightly so, but sometimes this protection came at too much of a cost.

There was a traditional religion in Nigeria, prior to Christianity and Islam. This involved all manners of herbal-based concoctions, potions and other strange stuff. The weirdest, most painful and most dangerous practice of this religion was something called 'Igbere' involving incisions made in your skin, using a very sharp blade followed by rubbing some sort of powder into the cuts.

According to traditional beliefs, the magical potions delivered into your blood streams through theses incisions would protect your from the evil imaginations that any of your enemies had against you. The biggest fear they protected you from was that of death. There is no doubt in my mind that all manners of infections were transferred between people and any possible unexplained deaths would be seen as the potion not being effective rather than potentially being the cause of an infectious disease.

As a child you felt the sharp blades as they made really quick cuts, you bled a bit and you felt the burning sensation as they rubbed the powder into an open and raw wound. Usually, you could get three, seven, and fourteen or even up to twenty-one incisions however there was no science behind it and all was dependent on the 'medicine man'. Usually these cuts were made on the wrists, ankle and occasionally on the head.

One fateful day, my father had come back from visiting a medicine man. He called me in, as was the norm, and said I needed to have some of the incisions. Well this time the incisions were to be all the way round my head.

After about the tenth incision, I was sweating from the pain with the sweat going into the raw wounds and this made the pain worse. It seemed to go on for hours although I am sure it was more like minutes. I wept from the pain and the discomfort but I felt powerless.

At the end of it all, I was a wreck and afterwards I told my father that would be the last time I would ever allow myself to be subjected to such a barbaric act. I told him categorically that nothing would happen to me, that he needed to stop being afraid for my life and consequently he should never again go to a 'medicine man' or anyone else for that matter.

I believed there was a God, well at least I had been taught that in Sunday school, and consequently I believed that he would protect me if he truly existed. If what I had been taught was a lie, then, I thought, there was no point being afraid of the inevitable. Fundamentally I simply believed no other human being could harm me in the ways that my parents feared.

For whatever reason, what I said must have struck a chord with my father because he listened to me and that was the last time he ever expected me to take part in anything like that.

I liberated myself that day but more importantly, I learnt that I had a voice and that I had a choice to use it to say 'no' to the things I did not want and 'yes' to the ones that I did.

I know it is not always easy to speak up, but that day pain and frustration gave me the push I needed to reject a barbaric custom as a young girl of eight.

I guess we all have to find the motivation that helps us to find and use our voice. Some are meant to liberate others so we need to buckle in and saddle up because of those who need us to say yes and no for them.

I am ever so grateful that because my father listened to me, he gave me my voice and I have never been afraid to use it since.

There are times when I choose not to use it but it is always a conscious decision and one that is not based on fear.

I have not failed. I've just found 10,000 ways that won't work.

Thomas A. Edison

I learn that just because I am scared of failing it does not mean I should not try - what's the worst thing that can happen?

As my father approached his retirement, he began to speak more and more about having a business. He was not really the business-minded kind of guy but I reckon the need to make money was enough of a motivation for him.

Well, he found someone who made him some household knives and we had the difficult job of selling them in my mum's store. The knives were not in keeping with other things my mum sold so no one came in looking for them or expecting to find them. Customers came for their milk, drinks, bread, snacks and tea bags.

Every morning my mum would faithfully set up the box of knives making them very visible to shoppers. Slowly, we sold the odd knife now and again. It took forever for the knives to sell and we never ordered a fresh stock when we eventually ran out. We didn't manage to sell them all and a couple ended up in our kitchen and a few others ended up as gifts to friends.

Why is this a lesson? You might ask.

It is a lesson because my father tried something outside of his comfort zone and he was not afraid to fail. He gave it his best shot when he tried, on a daily basis, to flog the product to people convincing them of its durability and strength.

Now I know not all businesses succeed and not all ideas materialise as we expect them to but not being afraid to try is already a success in itself.

In writing this book, there were moments when I wondered who would buy it or read it and if anyone would care. I still wrote it, I am already successful just because I was not too afraid to do so.

Life grants nothing to us mortals without hard work.

Horace

I learn the importance of setting your children up for success –
'Girls before boys – legacy of educating children'.

My father always seemed to have a bias towards his girls in terms of our education. He did not appear to push my brother as much as he pushed me and often I thought it was very unfair of him to treat me differently.

It took a while before I got it but I got it in the end. It was about 'girl power'. Not in the 'Spice Girls' sort of way but in the true sense of the phrase. My father told me that usually girls can either have their beauty or brains working for them and in some cases, for the lucky ones, they have both.

In his mind beauty fades so why waste your youth on anything other than developing and building the 'brains'? In really crude terms my father would often say, "if you are getting money or favours from a man, using your body et al, or if you were getting paid for services rendered using your body as the means of delivery, what happens when that body gets old and there are younger bodies on the market?" One day the wrinkles and the lines would mean you don't command the same price if any at all. You have to know this was before Botox and it was easy to see how your brains could be built on for as long as you wanted but your body was more likely to deteriorate over time.

I learnt the lesson pretty quick, as his analogy was like having to listen to the birds and the bee's lesson from your father, useful but super embarrassing.

For the male species, my father often alluded to the fact that there were some motivations that came at key points in a man's life such as the need to care for his family, have a girl friend or get married.

He was of the opinion that most men would be forced to knuckle down and work hard when the need came, especially if they found out their dream girl was not happy to be visiting them at their mum's house and she would not say yes to a proposal if she could not see a rosy future for herself with such a husband.

My father concluded, rightly or wrongly, that it is never quite too late for the boys, or at least they have more time to get it right, compared to their female counterparts.

He said when a lady does not get it right she is forced to rely on a man to take her in and take care of her every day of her life. She never truly has the guarantee that she will be taken care of because she never worked on her capacity and her capability to be relevant in the relationship. She could be widowed, discarded, abandoned or, worse still, abused and she has no way out.

When he put it in these terms, I did not waste any time learning the lessons as the alternatives were too vivid and traumatic and it was never going to be my lot in life. I made sure of it with my dad's help of course.

Show me a person who doesn't make mistakes and I'll show you a person who doesn't do anything.

Leonard Rubino

I learn that no one is perfect, but we can all aim to do better.

Just before you conclude that he was perfect and never did a thing wrong, this story is to set the record straight. No one is perfect and no one truly has the ability to be so this is to help those people who put too much pressure on themselves or on others around them.

He had his own set ways and sometimes it was near impossible to change his views or mind but he always had a listening ear and was, at the very least, willing to hear you out.

One of his colossally misleading views was that all of his children had to study Medicine. This was his personal dream growing up. He wanted more than anything to be a doctor but all his earlier struggles in life meant that the dream could not be realised. By the time he was able to afford to go to University, he was married with two children and being able to provide for his family became more of a priority than pursuing the long route to becoming a doctor. Snippets of his stories showed us how much he wanted to be educated and the things he did to advance that dream.

The final dream of his was to become a medical doctor and although he did not realize it himself, he had a back up plan for achieving it – he resolved that every one of his children would study Medicine instead. What he didn't quite factor in to this thought process was the fact that his children might not want this career path.

Although we knew of our father's ambitions, he had raised us to think and have a mind of our own. I guess he did not realise that all those years of making us believe we could do anything we wanted in life could come back to haunt him.

The unraveling of his dreams started with my brother who, one day, told my father he was going to study computer science.

Daddy could not hide his disappointment and, I know, he shed some tears mourning for his lost dream.

Thank God for great friends who were not afraid to speak the truth. My father went to tell one of them the disappointing news and he, in turn, help him see the error of his ways. He told daddy about the future of computers but, more importantly, he reminded him to trust the investments he had made in us.

Daddy came back home feeling a lot better and began, as he does in such circumstances, to research the field of computer science. Soon he knew enough about the subject and the potential opportunities it opened up that he became an advocate of the course. He never, after that day, showed any bias against my brother's chosen field of study but I guess, at the back of his mind, he always thought – there was still me.

It takes a while for some lessons to be learnt as my father again focused his attention on me becoming a doctor even though I could not stand to see people in pain. He would again be disappointed as I chose to study Business Administration. I did not know how to tell him my decision and break his heart so I played my cards close to my chest for as long as I could.

By the time I told him the course I applied for, he was devastated even though it was just two years after my brother's decision. He went back to his, friend who again told him to let his children follow their own paths and create their own destiny. I don't think it was hard for him to let me pursue my dream but he needed to express his disappointment to someone other than us. He embraced my course quickly and put me in touch with a friend of his who was a professor in my chosen field.

Looking back I don't think he would have been any prouder of us if we had become doctors.

You would have thought that by now he had learnt his lesson, not at all; he still had the same expectation of my two younger sisters who ended up studying Business Administration and Agricultural Economics respectively.

Until he died, I don't think he ever gave up on the idea of his children going into Medicine but what he chose to do was celebrate our accomplishments and brag about our academic achievements.

Years later he would admit he was glad that he let all off us pursue our own paths in life as he could see that we were all financially independent, fulfilled and happy which was all he ever wanted for us. His mistake was thinking that the only way we could achieve that was by going down the path he had chosen for us.

As his children we understood where this was coming from, we felt for his loss, disappointments and his struggles and our decisions not to study Medicine were not made lightly nor were they made without a sense of guilt but, more than anything, we knew we had to be strong enough to fight for our own convictions.

The blessing of it all was that he had taught us well even if the most important stand was going to be one against him.

We should be careful to get out of an experience only the wisdom that is in it – and stop there; lest we be like the cat that sits down on a hot stove-lid. She will never sit down on a hot stove-lid again – and that is well; but she will never sit down on a cold one anymore.

Twain, Mark

I learn that parents get it wrong too but they can learn to do better too.

"Forgiveness is the fragrance that the violet sheds on the heel that has crushed it".

Twain, Mark

I guess, my father, more than anyone else, knew that parents could be wrong too. He told us this story, which has resonated with me for over four decades. His mum gave birth to four sons and, it was said of the last child, that he was academically gifted, someone you would call a genius these days.

He gained admission to study Medicine in a top university and was on track to get a first class degree. As my father was the oldest son, he was always in dialogue with his mum about the future of all his brothers. He wanted them all to go to school and was willing to pay for their school fees even though he was a student as well.

Given the fraught relationship with his mother, his opinions were not always welcome. My father felt that this mum was indulging his two younger brothers by letting them skip school, not work hard on their grades or anything else they committed to. His mother shielded his brothers from any challenge and, at one point, she told my father that not all children were meant to go to school and have an education.

Education flowed in my father's veins and he would not have any of this. He kept paying for his brothers to go to school and they kept dropping out or using the money he worked so hard to send to them on things they were more interested in.

One day, the discussions got to a head and his mum told him that if he was worried about helping out his brothers later in life, he should stop, because her youngest son would help his older brothers.

Unfortunately this kind of thinking – that someone else would bear your responsibilities in life while you merely cruised along without feeling the pressure to pull your own weight – pervaded our society at the time and still does to some extent.

My father was disappointed at his mum's response but could do nothing. He subsequently tried to get his brothers to study some trades and one of them eventually trained to be a carpenter while the other one trained to be a bricklayer but, with my father's constant support, they should have achieved more than they did in life.

As they say, in life you never quite know what is right around the corner. For my grandmother, the most devastating and unimaginable horror happened unexpectedly when her youngest son died in his sleep in his final year of university, days before his final exams.

This was not just the death of a son; it was the death of a hope that the one son would make up for everything and everyone that was not good enough, in her eyes. His two older brothers suddenly had their 'meal ticket' snatched away and for the first time everyone saw what my father had been trying to tell them. Not a lot changed after that as my father continued to do what he could for his family. Unfortunately it was never enough as there was no way a single person, who himself was on a limited salary, could bear the cost of maintaining his own family, two others and his mother as well.

Growing up it was sad to see the consequences of poor parenting and bad choices but more importantly I think some of these underlying factors meant there was no love lost between the family and this is something that seems to have leaked in to the next generation.

For as long as I knew my father, his attitude towards his family never changed from that of love and compassion which meant that he provided for them throughout his life. He endeavored to do everything he could and sometimes he felt forced to put their needs ahead of ours.

Our mum always managed to bridge the financial gaps at such times. For many years, I was hurt on his behalf and could not imagine how he could forget everything he been through.

His ability to forgive and carry on against all odds is the single most important lesson he left behind in my opinion. I strive daily to be able to forgive in that way but even I know it is a tall order.

He took from the pain of his life only that which would help him and his family.

There are three things, which are real: God, human folly, and laughter. The first two are beyond our comprehension. So we must do what we can with the third.

Kennedy, John F.

I learn to explore all options and not to give up on people too quickly.

When my two younger sisters were in primary school, the older one decided to start wearing waist beads.

For those wondering why this is a big deal, having beads on your waist makes a woman feel really sexy. There is a heightened consciousness, as you walk, of those beads moving to the rhythm of your hips as they wiggled as though to unheard music. With beads on your waist you were more likely to sashay rather than just walk.

The beads would make any woman conscious of their sensuality and this is not a bad thing for a grown up who can handle the consequences but for a young girl, this was a major concern.

The younger sister knew about the beads and declared she didn't want any part of it but her opinion fell on deaf ears with the older one insisting that the only way dad would know was if she told on her. Adamantly, she went ahead with her 'waist beading' and, as expected, she was no longer free in the house; she was always reluctant to change her cloths without the doors being locked, which was odd and unexpected. At a point, she even moved out of their bedroom into the 'box room'. All of this had been going on for a couple of days and, though they didn't realise it, Dad had observed some of the recently odd behavior.

Usually, they queued to have a bath in the house, as it was a fairly large one with shared facilities. Daddy would wake them up early enough to bathe before the others got out of bed and that strategy worked well.

One morning however, Dad woke them up later than usual, which led to a rush and while hurrying to leave the house on time, to everyone's dismay, the beads came rolling down the waist.

Dad was not shocked, as far as anyone could tell but a few days later, he called the younger one and, in his usual manner, spoke analytically and critically to her about her sister's priorities. He said it baffled him that she had such distractions and poor choices on her mind at that tender age. It was such a long talk that my sister dozed and woke up a couple of times before it was over.

She began to wonder why she was the one listening to the lecture from hell. "Am I the one with the beads? Did I place them on her?" she asked herself.

She eventually challenged him … "Daddy, why am I the one you are talking to?"

He answered, "Because your character is questionable and your opinion is faulty." Whoever watches his brother go to the pit without calling him to order or seek help and guidance for him is responsible for the doom in that pit".

Those words struck her and they stuck like glue.

My father felt she did not do enough to help her sister see reason and do the right thing. This taught my sister not to give up on others too quickly and to ensure all options were explored before walking away from anyone going down the wrong path.

When she told me this story years later, I would learn the same lesson.

Only dead fish go 'with the flow'.

Unknown

I learn that the places I visit and the company I keep can affect my choices in life.

After the older of my younger sisters went to college and it was just Dad and the youngest, they moved to a first floor apartment. The apartment was more spacious, lovely and serene. My sister often referred to it as 'the place to be'.

Once a week, Daddy would take her out in the evening to a beer garden, the equivalent of a British pub. He would buy pepper-soup, a local delicacy, for her and watch her enjoy it, for the most part, not ordering anything for himself.

He would talk to her, as they sat there, and observed the customers' drunken behaviour and interactions. She told me she could still remember him saying, "Do you see all these men that get drunk? They are irresponsible. In life, it is unlikely you will meet a good husband in this kind of place, so be careful in the future. You see these ladies that hang around here aimlessly, laughing at the jokes of these drunken men – they have low morals and poor values. If you don't want to end up like these ladies that men touch disrespectfully, you have to be dedicated to your studies."

All those times, as my father carried on, she concentrated more on the pepper soup than on the talks, as those words had become overly familiar. Over time, she even started those conversations before him once they got there. Once the pepper soup was brought to the table, she would start by saying, "hmmnnn ... dad, I will study hard so I won't end up with low morals'.

Many years later, those life lessons would eventually make a lot more sense to her.

The frequency with which they went to the beer parlour reduced. One day, the owner of the beer garden saw them as they were approaching and she greeted them saying, "Sir, we have not been seeing you again, you'd better keep coming and forget your troubles at home!"

Daddy was very angry. He made a U-turn right there and then and, as they drove off, the woman and the others pleaded with them that it was a joke but Dad didn't respond and that was the last time they ever went there. My father was principled like that.

When she asked him why he reacted the way he did, he said, "Whoever tries to run away from his troubles will never get the solution to them."

Then she said to him, "but Daddy, we don't have any troubles" and he answered, "it is not so much that we don't have troubles but that we would have gotten the wrong counsel if we actually had some".

He went on to comment that the Bible says we should stay away from ungodly counsels. "Besides" he said, "I have delivered the message I wanted to pass across. Now you know everything I told you, while we went there, by heart. There is no need to push any further".

It was then she realized, it was never about having a great time enjoying the food and drink; those times were meant to get a key message across. He took her there to see the kind of woman she should not be and to see the kind of men she should never be found with.

She said she just kept wondering as they drove home about the kind of man that our father was, a man that would demonstrate a lot of initiative and creatively come up with scenarios and props to help get a life lesson across.

Funnily enough, I believe anyone who ever met my father would have at one time or another wondered the same thing. He tended to have that effect on the people he came across.

There are no secrets to success. It is the result of preparation, hard work, and learning from failure

Colin Powell

I learn to believe in myself and in my abilities.

As daddy was a head teacher, we often moved with his job. After my brother and I had left home for college, the rest of the family moved to a new town.

At this time my two younger sisters were the only ones at home. The older was going into her last year of primary school and daddy took them to the best school he had found in the new town.

The school was a private nursery and quite expensive but he was willing to pay for the quality. Admission to the school was quite stringent and they automatically disqualified the older one based on the fact that she was in the final year.

I guess in their opinion, they were concerned that they had not had the opportunity to shape her education previously and obviously they did not realise how much shaping she had had from our father.

They gave daddy the option of her repeating a year instead of joining the final class, but he refused and told the headmistress that he knew the quality of the child he had raised. He insisted that they at least interview her but they said no due to their policy.

He asked the woman to recommend a public school that was local to their residence. The lady looked perplexed but she checked the school lists and gave a name of a local Baptist school.

Daddy then told her that he would take my sister to the public school and that he was sure that she would beat any pupil from her private school at the common entrance examinations. He said he would prove to her that my sister was made up of a quality and unique pedigree.

The woman seemed out of her comfort zone and she apologised for the policy. In the meantime, the younger one was scheduled for her own test and interview. Daddy called her aside and told her to be confident. He advised her not to panic because he knew she could do better than anyone around there. He told her to answer like 'my father's daughter'. He said, "You have all the answers in your head, just dish them out" He then gave her "high 5", saying "make me proud, show me off".

'My father's daughter' was a phrase he had coined that reminded us that we were special and could do anything, whenever I heard that I felt on top of the world, unstoppable and that anything was possible. Years letter, he was still using the phrase to inspire my sisters.

As a young girl my sister's morale was instantly boosted and it shot up through the roof when she heard my father say this. She went in, did the written examinations and passed. Immediately they saw her name, on the noticeboard where the results were posted, dad said, "Can you see now?"

Then it was time for the interview. The interview wasn't a bog standard one like the ones she had done previously. There were mathematical questions to solve and quickly. She had to come up with a way to allow her time to figure out the answers.

Her strategy was simple and brilliant. Well at least it seemed like that to her. She simply repeated the question back to the examiner. What is 9x7? She would say … "9x7. Simple question! Answer is 63." By simply repeating the question, she allowed herself the thinking time before she responded correctly. It all went well and the interviewer said, "She is so confident! Brilliant one!"

She smiled all the way to Daddy and as they drove home, all they did was talk about her strategy and they just laughed endlessly. He let her talk about it for as long as she needed to and he never stopped laughing. Each time she went over it, he laughed as though he was hearing it for the first time. That is the kind of father he was.

He humoured us for as long as we were happy to go on. He loved to make us laugh, sometimes he laughed at us but he mostly laughed with us.

Experience is a grindstone; and it is lucky for us, if we can get brightened by it, and not ground.

Josh Billings

I learn about patience and get to know that life is filled with moments that require the right choices to be made and each new opportunity needs to be embraced fully.

My youngest sister told me about a time when she was in a new school and after school finished, she went to the agreed pick up point. She saw his RED Peugeot 504 but didn't see him in the car so she stayed at a safe distance and checked the car plate number again ... KW 5600 A!

It was the right car but the man in the car was not my father. What she did not realise was that the man was my father's new official driver. Being security conscious and remembering the steer from my father about going with strangers, she chose to walk rather than approach the stranger just because he had the right car. Kidnapping was an issue and the car could easily have been stolen so it was the right move on her part.

It was a long way home so she decided to go to his friend's office, as this was closer. She knew he was one of my dad's trusted and best friends and he was often in our house, actually it was more like on a daily basis. She walked there and the driver went back to my dad when he didn't see her.

His friend bought popcorn and peanuts for her and gave her a lift home. On the way, they met my dad's car and flagged him down. He was so grateful to his friend for the help and he told them that it was a test, as he wanted to know if she was able to think on her feet and make a good decision. He actually made a bet with his colleagues and the new driver that his daughter would not get into his car if he was not the one behind the wheel.

As one would expect, she was so glad that she passed the test and everyone commended her.

After about a month, school finished and she expected to meet Daddy waiting to pick her up but he wasn't there. She waited for a couple of minutes and off she went to his friend's office again.

She was only there for a few minutes before daddy showed up and he greeted everyone cheerfully, thanking the staff members for looking after her again and she left the office with him.

When they got outside, he told her she had just failed a test; that he actually came late to see how long she would patiently wait for him before dashing off to his friend's office.

She told me that the worst part of the scold was when he asked if the snacks they gave her the last time was the reason that she couldn't wait to be there again.

She felt bad because the first time she was there, she only reluctantly took the snacks when they gave her and she would have chosen not to tell him if she knew he would bring it up in the future. She did not consider for one moment that it would come back to haunt her.

When they got back to the car, to her surprise, the next thing daddy did was to get in and lock the doors. Refusing to open the door for her, he started the engine, wound down the side window and told her it would be odd for her to go back in there requesting help having just left the same building with him. She was bewildered, wondering what in heavens was going on.

She thought it was a joke until he waved telling her they would see at home real soon. She stood there staring at him, watching him leave, not quite fully comprehending what the big deal was.

She quickly walked out of the car park and it was such a long trek home because his friend's office was in the opposite direction from her school. She walked back past her school and as she did she could only imagine why she didn't wait patiently for just a couple of minutes.

It was one of those moments that you wished you had made

a different split second decision. I guess it is the same as the thoughts on a driver's mind when their car is hit because they made a split second hasty and foolish decision that eventually costs them hours of inconvenience and money.

Well the journey home began for her as she trekked and trekked for what seemed like an eternity and when she finally got home, she saw daddy taking a pretend nap. He welcomed her, told her to go eat the food he had prepared and turned to the wall continuing his pretend nap, but not before she saw the corner of his lips curving in a faint smile.

Only God knows what he was thinking. Usually you can't gather too much from the expressions on his face.

That day she learnt an unforgettable lesson – the great virtue called Patience! I also learnt this lesson when she told me the story.

My father wanted her to know that just because she made a choice on one occasion that was appropriate, did not mean that it would still be the right choice in another situation and she needed to weigh every situation based on its own merit and make an informed decision. That's a lesson worth knowing.

Every day do something that will inch you closer to a better tomorrow.

Doug Firebaugh

I learnt about contentment and not coveting what others have.

My youngest sister told me about a time when there was an end of year party in their school and Daddy was the chairperson. One of the highlights was a performance of a local dance and the older sister was meant to be in the cultural dancing troupe and needed some special costume for the event.

Mummy would quite often initially say you couldn't have something when you ask for it even though she would eventually give you. We all knew this about her and would just give her time to change her mind. She took good care of the few special clothes she had so it was understandable that her initial reaction was to not be frivolous with them.

My sister asked for a special fabric and mum was reluctant to give her. She also needed traditional beads, which she didn't have. At the last minute before leaving home for school, mum rummaged through her suitcases for the special fabric but my sister already had a picture of what she wanted for the occasion and had decided that nothing my mum had was fashionable enough. She reluctantly took what Mummy had for her but unknown to them she had already figured out what she was going to do.

The big day came and the cultural dance troupe performed to everyone's delight with her in the forefront, completely transformed. People sat next to my father were telling him how well his daughter danced. He could not believe his eyes that it was his daughter looking all decked up in clothes he did not recognise and could not have afforded. He laughed and even clapped for her. When they got home, he told her she was the most gorgeous, glamorous and graceful in the dance and she was pleased with herself.

Suddenly, the story turned around when he sat them down

and told her it was inappropriate for her to have borrowed clothing just to keep up with the Jones'. She had taken the clothes my
mum gave her giving everyone the impression she would wear
the clothes but resorted to her back up plan. Daddy referred to it
as the height of covetousness. He talked and talked and talked as
usual and they just sat there wondering why her greatest cheer-
leader on the field turned to be her biggest critic in the privacy
of their own home.

As usual the younger one could not keep her mouth shut!
And told him, "But daddy, you clapped for her there".

He said, "it is better for you to cover your brother's shame
outside than be ridiculed with him in the market square".

She learnt two invaluable lessons, firstly to be proud of who
she was and what she could afford and secondly there was a
right time and place to address issues.

These lessons resonated with me as she shared the story and
I continue to work them out in my life, glad that I got to keep
learning from my father years after I left home.

The whole of life is but a moment of time. It is our duty, therefore to use it, not to misuse it.

Plutarch

I learn there is no such thing like "I can't do without something or someone".

Daddy once told me a story about a family friend. This happened when they lived in a city called Zaria in the northern part of Nigeria. He said the lady was a lover of meat and took pride in it. She was known to say she could not live life without meat and could never get tired of meat.

Saying this persistently in front of my dad was like waving a red flag in from of a wild bull. Not willing to disappoint anyone, he said he resolved within himself to prove to her that she had a wrong notion and also show her there was nothing spectacular about meat.

One day, he gave her one pound, which was a lot of money in those days, and told her to get different cuts of meat for him. It was a lot of meat and he asked for her help to cook it and while she was cooking, she was busy tasting away. At the end of the cooking, he then told her to join him in eating. She soon pushed the meat aside saying she did not feel like having any more meat. My father reminded her of her claim that she could never have too much meat and that this was her opportunity to have as much as she wanted and that she could even take some home.

As they tasted different cuts of meat, she said she would be glad if she never saw another piece of meat for a good while. Daddy said that was how he put an end to her craving for meat and she was a changed woman from that day. It wasn't about the meat as it could have been any other craving. He wanted to show her that she had a choice and the power within her to exercise her choice including managing any cravings.

When I asked why he did that, he said he wanted her and the people around to know there is no such thing like "I can't do without something or someone".

It didn't make much sense to me until he used the same approach in another event years later. We had two cousins staying with us who were always fighting. Usually, they behaved themselves when Daddy was around but he knew they quarreled constantly and had become a nuisance to the neighbours.

However, the day he decided to address the issue was when he saw them fighting inside a shop from across the street. Daddy didn't say much; he just came around and told them to clear the sitting room. No one knew what he was up to until he called both of them inside.

He told them he had created a space seeing as they clearly wanted to fight. That was how the rumble began! We all thought it was a joke. The fight moved from the sitting room to the hallway, back to the room, and then out again and into the last room. This fight was on for what seemed like ages but was more like a few minutes and at some point, they had even pulled off each other's clothes, sweating and panting, the hot climate not helping matters.

Soon enough, they were losing steam and he asked if they were ready to keep on fighting the 'good fight' or stop 'fighting for good'. By the time they decided that they were done fighting for good, they had exhausted all their energy. That was the last day they fought in our house and it seemed like the rest of us were scared that it may be our turn so we all learnt not to fight or argue unnecessarily.

It was a peaceful new dawn.

Then he told us, "when you give people more than enough of what they think they want, you are able to douse their insatiable quest for it or at least help them put it into perspective".

One way to get the most out of life is to look upon it as an adventure.

William Feather

I learn, there is a right time for everything.

The next story is just a simple one about an event that happened when my youngest sister was only seven years old.

One day, daddy told her to pronounce every thing they came across. She was meant to say it out loud. Every word, every time, wherever!

At the same time, they had also started taking turns to be on a chore roster in the house and each person on duty was also expected to give a detailed report of the activities that went on during that whole day. Starting from the moment they woke up to when the lights were put out at night. He gave them a journal where they wrote about the chores and everything else that happened during the day.

To her it was a bit like a game, but for daddy, there is always a point to every game and a lesson to be learnt on every 'supposed' fun stroll.

There was a day she saw an invitation card and on reading it saw it was addressed to the 'Inutorise' family and she pronounced it as In – u – to – rise. He clapped for her while everyone else laughed knowing that it was a Nigerian name with a whole different pronunciation. Daddy simply called her aside and told her she was right and everyone else wrong.

Another day he asked her the meaning of Grandmother and Grandfather and she said it means mummy and daddy's groundnut respectively. He clapped for her saying she was absolutely correct.

One day he asked her to share something with her big sister and when she refused he told her she was selfish. She didn't understand but wasn't bothered telling him, "I don't sell fish" and he just let her be.

Much later as she got older and got to know the meanings of

these words, she asked him why he gave her the impression that she was right all those times and he told her that it was the time he was teaching her compound words and he wasn't about to mess up her head when she was right in the given context.

That, to me, is a Teacher! He taught in the most unusual ways and never missed an opportunity to impart wisdom, insight and knowledge.

Life is a succession of lessons which must be lived to be understood.

Ralph Waldo Emerson

I learn it's not just about the end goal, the lessons on the journey are equally important.

When my youngest sister was in the fifth year in primary school she and my dad moved to a new village and it was just the two of them at this time.

Dad had started giving her some of the responsibility of making dinner for them. He taught her to make 'Eba' a Nigerian delicacy that looks like mashed potato. To prepare it, you need boiling water and some ground cassava flour. There was an art to it, too much water and it was sloppy, too little water and it was hard as a rock but to an expert, it is one of the simplest dishes to learn as you grow up.

She had attempted it a couple of times but no matter how hard she tried each time the right consistency and texture of the food eluded her. Even though it was usually too soft, daddy would always eat it saying it was nice but she knew it wasn't.

One day she decided to change the order of the cooking process deciding to put in the cassava flour first into the bowl and then pour the boiling water on it. The water went in just a bit far but apparently not all the way down. She touched it and the top felt hard enough, commending her own effort, she thought Hurray!

Daddy also touched it later on and said that it looked well done so he picked a spoon to turn it and the dried cassava flour came flying out from below the surface. She expected him to be disappointed but he just started laughing and told her what she had done wrong. He then proceeded to measure a bowl of boiling water and told her the number of cups of the flour that would make a perfect meal and that was the magic.

She considers herself an expert at making the food now. What she learnt that day is that it was not so much about the food, it was all about a man who would offer praise for effort even when it was not done perfectly.

I was not surprised when she told me this story as my brother and I lived through similar versions growing up as my father taught us about the value of making an effort even when the final outcome falls short of expectations.

Time and tide wait for no man.

Geoffrey Chaucer

I learn to never waste an opportunity to recognise, praise and appreciate people.

Back then Daddy used to make moin-moin, another Nigerian delicacy made from black eyed beans blended with onions, red peppers, seasoning and olive oil. On more special occasions, fish, prawns and chopped boiled eggs were added to enrich it. The batter is then wrapped in banana leaves, which give it a unique flavour. Some people would wrap it in a plastic bag but this lacked the unique traditional and authentic taste.

Daddy always made it with banana leaves but my sister never got to start the process with him as she always came back from school to meet him halfway through making it. She wanted to surprise him one day by making the moin-moin before he got back so she started on it getting all her preparations done quickly.

There is an art to using banana leaves to wrap the mixture as it was quite runny and the leaves could easily split with the contents spilling out into the pan. A lot of people would struggle to use these leaves often taking the easy route out resorting to using plastic bags or tins to cook it.

My sister started grappling with the banana leaves but they kept leaking. Whenever she thought she had got a hang of one, gingerly placing it in the boiling water, lo and behold, it would leak into the pot causing the water to bubble up. Her nice little parcels were becoming mushy right before her eyes and she was frustrated to no end.

Daddy came back and saw this. He asked her to shake his hands for a job well done saying the attempt was enough food for him. He asked her to prepare another batch, and then showed her how to tenderize the banana leaves over some heat to soften them making them easier to fold and twist before using them to steam the delicately spiced bean mixture. She watched him do the first one then he watched her do the rest.

That was a great day for her and I was told the moin-moin was delicious.

For me I learnt that in life, you don't have to be perfect to be praised and it is important to celebrate every milestone and praise every accomplishment during life's pursuit of excellence.

Take care of the minutes and the hours will take care of themselves.

Lord Chesterfield

I learn nothing is lost in the process of learning – failure is all about knowing what not to do the next time around.

I remember a time when my aunt came home to spend the weekend with dad and I. It was her first visit as she had just gained admission to a local college. As she was around, dad asked her to make pounded yam, which was a special treat as dad worked away from home and the only other opportunity to eat a proper home-made version would be when we visited the rest of the family.

Pounded yam is a local delicacy served with meat and vegetable sauce and it was massively popular with many Nigerian tribes. It was made by cooking tubers of yam and using a wooden mortar and pestle to pound it until it was well kneaded together with no lumps. Hot water was added to achieve the right texture and consistency. Too much water and it would be too soft, too little water it would be difficult to swallow. Knowing how to make great pounded yam was a rite of passage and you had to have perfected it by the time you got married otherwise your in-laws would mock your ability to take care of your family. Not knowing how to make it is similar to a chef not knowing how to make a puff pastry

My aunt had lived with us before going off to college and didn't do any cooking as my mum did all of it herself. The only way to really learn what to do in the kitchen was to keenly observe my mum and hope that your knowledge pulls through for you when you attempt to cook in the future

Although my aunt had never cooked pounded yam before she agreed to my dad's request. She pounded the yams a couple of times and poured in water while daddy watched her. When my aunt realized that the mixture wasn't kneading together as it ought to, dad walked up to her and asked if everything was fine. It obviously wasn't and you could see from her face that she knew her attempt was a woeful one.

Dad told her to throw the batch away and start from scratch by peeling and cooking another batch of yams. The next set turned out the same as the earlier one and it too ended up in the bin. Dad asked her to try again, noting what had not worked previously. She persevered until she mastered the art on her fourth attempt.

That was Daddy's unique approach to learning. He did not care about the number of yams that were wasted or the time that was lost; he was not bothered that he was hungry – as far as he was concerned it was more important for my aunt to learn how to cook, and that she did. She learnt by figuring out what was not working.

Spare moments are the gold dust of time.

Bishop Hail

I learn some things are more important than money.

Daddy never wasted an opportunity to teach us lessons and one that was really poignant was on the back of a tragedy. It was about the only time my sister saw him really devastated.

She came home from school that fateful day and saw him sitting in the sitting room. Her food was ready but his was not there. That was strange because he always set a table for the two of them. She kept stealing glances at him, as his grief was palpable.

When he saw that she was getting concerned and that she was looking at him with confusion written all over her face, he told her that our uncle had died in a plane crash. That was the first time Daddy ever took half a day off work. He told her, young as she was, that anybody could die at any time. He said that death did not have consideration for a person's age.

The alarming part of the story was when he said that when he dies, she should hold close to her heart all the words he had ever said to her, as she heard more from him than anyone else being the last child.

He told her she almost had it all together and that if she followed all he had been saying to her, she was bound to turn out fine in life, no matter how challenging things got to be.

By this he meant he had almost finished imparting the knowledge and wisdom he wanted to share with her. He always considered what else he might want to teach his children and we all think he kept some sort of mental statistics of what he still had left to teach each of us. For those of us who lived away from home, he would write letters to us and offer rich words of wisdom.

As my sister sat there staring at him, she wondered in her young mind whether he was going to die the following day. He said to her, "when I die, all you will be left with are my words to you. I do not have one brick laid on another anywhere on earth."

This was his way of reminding her that he was not leaving financial wealth and properties behind for any of us to inherit. He often said that he was investing everything in us while he was still alive.

That night, my sister said she couldn't sleep as she kept thinking what she would do in such a large house if he died.

While he did not leave much money when he passed away, he left each of us with enough determination, courage and wisdom to accomplish and fulfill every dream and desire he had for us or that we had for ourselves.

Thrift of time will repay you in after-life with a thousandfold of profit beyond your most sanguine dreams.

William E. Gladstone

I learn just because you are having fun doesn't mean you should forget who you are or what your ideals are.

As told by my younger sister:

There was a time I lived with my father in a grand house. A man who worked as a company director owned it and offered it to my father because he had built himself a mansion elsewhere in the village. The house we occupied was also massive by any standard and it was well built and decorated.

Initially I was not allowed to go out but after a while, I was permitted to make friends with our landlord's daughter. On one particular day, they came around to visit and I was allowed, unusually, to go and play in their mansion, which was not too far away.

For someone who, at the time, did not have access to a television, it was quite a treat walking into a cinema room with everything you could wish for. I began to watch a film and I soon got carried away, not knowing how much time had elapsed. Hours flew by and eventually my beloved father asked someone to come get me and I instantly knew there was trouble!

I went home, fully ready to face the music. He welcomed me asking me to eat. I ate and marveled at his magnanimity. I knew I deserved a talking to, knowing full well that I had abused his trust in me.

After I had finished my dinner, he gave me, what I can only describe as, a grand telling off. It was more like verbal diarrhea filled with his opinions about my behaviour.

Afterwards, the only reason I didn't ask him why he gave me food first was because I knew what his answer would be. He knew that if he told me off first, I would lose my appetite and that would mean going to bed hungry. This was something he hated passionately. To avoid this, he would keep his emotions in check until our tummies were full and then we got whatever 'lecture' was coming.

I learnt that day to never be sidetracked by life's little pleasures. They are meant to be enjoyed and not take over our lives distracting us from our own goals.

Love nothing but that which comes to you woven in the pattern of your destiny. For what could more aptly fit your needs?

Marcus Aurelius

I learn that you don't have to pretend to be like the Jones's because charting your own course is within your reach.

As told by my younger sister:

When we lived in the millionaire's house, I was doing so well in my academics and, given his daughter and I had developed a close friendship, her father suggested that he could sponsor my secondary education.

He offered my father a scholarship so that I could go to a top secondary school, which in fact was the flagship school in the country at the time. It was very well known and children of the rich and famous were in attendance there.

I had never been so excited. That school was it! I was so disappointed when my dad told me his take on the situation. I thought it was a joke. He went to thank the man and declined his offer.

He gave the excuse that he didn't want me to go to secondary school just yet as I was still immature and he would want me to get through the sixth year of my primary education. As I am quite vocal, I wanted to ask him why he was taking such an unreasonable stance. After some time, I became less angry and he explained that it would be highly irresponsible for him to put me in a school he could not afford. The scholarship would not pay for everything and he knew he could not afford the difference.

He said he didn't need a scholarship from another person just to put me in a social class to which I did not belong. The school was very 'elite' and not meant for people like us – people who needed to be grounded in life; people who would have to work for every success they would have. A lot of attendees of the school were born with silver spoons in their mouth and they weren't always in class to learn, more to have the credentials that matched their family's wealth and status.

He did however say, that whichever school I went to, the most important thing was for me to be able to compete with the other kids, from all the other schools, including the elite ones. He needed me to know and prove to them that the school doesn't make a student – the student makes the school. Despite all of this, I was still sad.

He said he wanted to be able to stand up, beat his chest and say in public, "I brought up my child, come see where she is today."

We spoke at length. As usual, he won and I just had to let go of the silver spoon that was being offered to me. When I look back now, I think of my father as a principled man and, while you may not agree with his views, you can't deny that he always had the best interest of his family at heart.

The first step in the acquisition of wisdom is silence, the second listening, the third memory, the fourth practice, the fifth teaching others.

Solomon Ibn Gabriol

I learn that things aren't always as they seem and everyone deserves to be given the benefit of the doubt.

This is not an easy story for me to tell but I am telling it because it has learning points for everyone.

One day we were at home and a woman came knocking on our door. She happened to be an old friend of Daddy's. He told me that he had dated her many years ago, when he first started teaching and even thought back then that they were going to get married someday.

Well, I only found this out after the fact but you would need to know how we got to this key piece of information.

She was welcomed and she told us how she found out where daddy worked and lived. She said she was in the nearby town for a screening in an office when she heard some people talking and his name came up, following a bit of probing, she ascertained that they were talking about the same person she had known all those years ago.

She decided to stop by our house the following day on her way back home. We made food, she ate and because it was too late to catch a bus home, she had to stay the night so daddy asked me to get the other room ready for her. This I did grudgingly because I was wondering why we had to accommodate a strange woman. I didn't know her before and I was yet to know her story and her previous connection with my father. He could see that I was very cold towards them but he never said a word.

While I was preparing the room, I picked up a piece of cardboard and cut it into a card size. I picked up some markers and colouring crayons and began to draw. What I was doing was so surreal that it felt like an out of body experience, and all this while, only God knew what I was doing.

This was about the time that the awareness of HIV/AIDS was

intensifying and the symbol was the human skull and two long bones crossing each other to make a symbol of an X.

I drew this picture on the front of the card and wrote some words in it. Some of them as I recall were that:

- AIDS is Real!
- Your family needs you.
- Your family loves you.
- Adultery is wrong. Resist it.
- I love you, my daddy.

I signed this card with my initial and last name placing the card in the wardrobe where I knew he would have to pick the robe that he sleeps in.

I waited, resisting every urge to go to sleep early as they talked. I was intent on keeping an eye on them. I began to doze off and daddy urged me to turn in for the night but I refused. I made sure I saw the woman go to her room and I stealthily followed her with the intention of locking her in it. I noticed my dad get up to get his eye drops so I hid until he passed by.

Daddy and I shared a room as the other one was occupied so I waited to make sure he came back inside. Apparently, he had seen my supposed greeting card but never said anything.

I drifted off to sleep and the following morning, I woke up very angry because I had not succeeded in locking her in and keeping the key as I had planned. When I got to the sitting room, Daddy was there but the woman was still asleep. I didn't greet him because I was so angry.

As I went to sit down, he asked how I was but I didn't answer so he kept quiet as well. When the woman finally came down to the sitting room I did not greet her either and refused to respond when she greeted me. I stayed moody.

I left the sitting room to brush my teeth and as I was coming back, daddy was coming up as well and we met on the staircase. Usually whenever our paths crossed in the house, he would tickle me and I would giggle in return, but that morning, he tickled me and I shoved his hands off so he did what he usually didn't do. He landed me a smack! I held my face, looked him in the eyes and asked what that was for but he just shook his head and left me there.

I went back to the room to sulk and cry!

Before long the woman was ready to go and she left for the bus station. Daddy asked me to see her off to the park and by the time I came back, he called me and said we had to talk.

I sat at the other end of the sofa to him and he had my card in his hands. He told me a lot of things that day and one of the lessons that stuck was that he didn't appreciate the fact that I was not courageous enough to ask questions when I was confused.

He told me that in life, when I have an opportunity to save people from making mistakes, I shouldn't pick the weakest means of doing that.

He said, assuming that he had wanted to commit adultery with the woman, he may not have seen the card, could have gone ahead and done it and by the time he saw the card, it would be too late.

He told me that in life I should stand up for what I believe and say it out loud, no matter the consequence, even if it means standing alone.

I then asked him why he smacked me and he explained that it was because I made him realise that I had not taken on board any of the lessons he had given me. He also reminded me that I was better than the attributes I had displayed with regards to how I related with the poor woman.

He said that he expected me to show her what fine young

woman he had raised me to be. He lamented that I didn't trust him and I did not ask him about it – I simply took a standpoint without hearing his part of the story. I sat there staring at him, appalled by my own behaviour.

He then told me about the woman, which is how I got to know about their previous history. He gave me some insight into what they were talking about the previous night.

I found out about how the woman suffered abuse at her husband's hand. Dad explained that even though he was sleepy, the least he could do for her was offer a listening ear with empathy and words of advice.

We ended up talking for a really long time as he told me how to handle marriage and past relationships.

All I could do was to listen to his 'sermons' as usual and then we went and rearranged our guest room back to how it was. Peace and calmness returned to our house while I had guilty feelings about how I was rude to the woman due to my impatience.

I learnt that day that things aren't always as they seem, people deserve the benefit of the doubt and, most importantly, if I feel strongly about something, I need to be bold and caring enough to own and air my concerns.

It might just save someone's life.

This is my sister's story told in her own words and when she shared it with me, I could empathise with all the parties. I could see how in her immaturity she was trying to protect my father, defend our mum but I could also see that this did not excuse her behaviour. The woman's story brought home some of the other lessons my father had been instilling in us as we were growing up.

A loving heart is the truest wisdom.

Charles Dickens

I learn about how much love he had for me and how he wanted me to have anything I desired in life.

As told by my younger sister:

Mummy was going for a wedding on a Saturday morning and I told her I wanted to eat yam and fried egg, but she said that I had to eat what had been prepared in the house. I was angry but I kept quiet; I went to sit in the living room and cry. Daddy came into the room and as usual he tried to play with me but then he noticed that I was upset.

He asked why and I told him what mummy had said to me. I could see the love of a father in his eyes and Daddy made sure I ate what I desired on that day.

Later he called me to the room and told me the reason he had worked hard all of his life was because his children were the centre of his world and he said anything I wanted on earth I would have. He wept that day and mum felt bad. His love for the family was simply incomparable.

Knowing is not enough; willing is not enough; we must do.

Johann Wolfgang von Goethe

I learn about friendship and choosing the right friends.

As told by my younger sister:

Friendship is a choice and not to be forced. My father often quoted a popular Nigerian proverb that says, "You shouldn't need a flashbulb to search for your family". This means it should not be too difficult to maintain relationship with a loved one, either a friend or a family member. And if you find yourself stressed about a relationship, then it is time to rethink your choices.

I remembered years back, when my younger sister used to go up to the next flat to play with our neighbour's daughter. She was still young, but she stopped going there when she came back from college. One day their daughter, her old playmate, came into our sitting room and they got talking about things that teenage girls talk about.

As my sister was telling her about life in boarding school it was obvious that her interest was in clothes, bags and other girlie stuff. She began to compare her mum's wardrobe to that of my mother. My sister was so upset because she made her feel like the clothes my mum had were not good enough. And this translated to her young mind feeling that she was saying her mum was better than ours. This upset my sister so much that she asked her to leave.

As she left, daddy came into the room to tell my sister that he was proud that she was able to make the right choice of removing herself from an upsetting situation by bringing it to an end.

He explained that this did not make her old playmate the enemy but at the same time she was not really her friend as her focus was now different as she viewed life from a whole other angle. He told my sister to focus on her studies and that in the future there was nothing that she would not be able to get for our mummy if she wanted.

And his perspective has now become the reality today; because of what the girl valued then and what dad taught us to value, there is a marked difference between our lives today.

The ultimate measure of a man is not where he stands in moments of comfort, but where he stands at times of challenge and controversy.

Martin Luther King, Jr.

I learn to always stand up for the truth and justice.

Daddy never kept quiet in the face of injustice and he couldn't tolerate people not standing up for the truth. He would always speak his mind even if that would end a friendship or relationship.

An incident that epitomised this happened to a young man who was visiting his uncle who lived across the street from us. Daddy spent a lot of time with his uncle and a few other men and they would discuss and debate the ills of society attempting to repair everything that was wrong with the nation. The news media fed them enough topics for each day's discussion.

One day there was a misunderstanding between the young man and a woman living in one of the flats on the lower floor. It was clear that the lady was at fault as people who stepped in to resolve the issue laid the blame at the lady's feet.

The woman would not have any of it and she went to the police station to report the young man. The police came and arrested the man and a couple of witnesses went along with him. The men told daddy to stay back as he was much older than them and they did not want to put any stress or physical strain on him. He did as he was advised.

Not quite ten minutes later daddy went into his room to change his clothes, collected some money from mummy and said he was going to the police station. My mum tried to stop him from going and threatened that she would not come to his rescue if the police for any reason detained him. Daddy simply nodded his head and left.

By the time daddy got to the police station, he found out that the young man had been locked up because the two witnesses did not tell the police exactly what had happened. They ended up supporting the lady so when daddy got there he asked the police why they had kept the young man who they now insisted was at fault.

Daddy proceeded to clarify the truth and said that he was surprised that the two men did not tell the police the true version of the event. Due to his boldness to stand up for the truth, the young man was released from lockup and the woman was arrested for perverting the course of justice. She was eventually released after much pleading from her and a stern warning from the police.

The police expressed their appreciation to daddy and said they were very grateful because he steered them towards the truth.

They quoted a Nigerian proverb that says, "An elder can not be in the market and watch the head of a baby hanging improperly and do nothing". This simply means that a mature person will restore order when necessary as they won't stand by and do nothing when a situation calls for an action.

Daddy stopped going across the street to spend time with his old buddies and they, in turn, were ashamed of their actions. The talk on the street was about how two grown men lied and that it was only through providence and sheer luck that my dad saved the day. After some weeks they started coming to our house to sit with daddy and he took the opportunity to let them know that what they had done was wrong.

I learnt that day the importance of having people of integrity around you especially when your life and destiny are at stake.

Exert your talents, and distinguish yourself,
and don't think of retiring from the world,
until the world will be sorry that you retire.

Samuel Johnson

Live in each season as it passes; breathe
the air, drink the drink, taste the fruit, and
resign yourself to the influences of each.

Henry David Thoreau

I learn to never rely on someone else's accomplishments, as it is more rewarding to work on having some yourself.

I never learnt to drive until I was twenty-four years old and owned my own car but my brother on the other hand could not wait to learn to drive and he was still in primary school when he showed a keen interest in driving and he could drive the car by the time he turned sixteen. My father was not too keen but eventually taught him to drive but he planned to hold back on getting him a license until he felt he was matured enough to handle it not becoming a distraction.

This is a lesson I learnt from my brother and I decided to share the story in his own words, so here it goes.

In my first year in university, we were on a break so I decided to travel to see daddy, as was the normal practice at the time. It was an opportunity to help him out at the farm, which he always ran on the side. He grew most of our food, there was always a lot of harvest and we ended up giving a fair bit away, occasionally even selling some of the crops.

Usually he paid for hired help to support him but whenever we were on a break at the university, he didn't need to hire labourers as I usually took up the responsibility to pick up the slack and save some money for the family. It wasn't as if I could work as hard as the labourers but "slow and steady wins the race." Daddy was always very appreciative of it.

One particular day one of his friends came from the city; I knew he could easily get to the licensing office, as there was no local office close to where we lived. Also I knew my father would not want me to get a driver's license at that time so I approached him to help me get a driver's license, without telling my father, and he obliged. Back then I was already very experienced in

174

driving, though without a license.

Somehow daddy found out about my request and, after the man left, he sat me down saying we had a matter to discuss. Of course I knew there was trouble from the way he approached the conversation. He was an open book and most times you could tell from a mile away if you were in his bad books.

He said, "I learnt you wanted to get a driver's license" and I said, "yes".

Then he said, "I was wondering why you needed it, are you planning to take up a vacation job as a commercial driver? I don't want to believe you are getting it for my vehicle, which is not yours. I will advise you to work hard to own your own car then get a license to drive it."

I was so upset at the time that I vowed never to drive his car again and for years I stood my ground refusing to drive the car.

Five years later when I started working, I was given an official car so I had to get a driver's license. It was such an exciting moment that the first person I called to break the news to was daddy.

I can still remember what he said when I gave him the fantastic news. He said, "it's more glorious and fulfilling this way, back then it would have amounted to living a false life."

I agreed with him at the time and when I look back now, I realise he was teaching me not to depend on someone else's trophies or accomplishments. Now when I look at the celebrity culture and I see so many young people hanging around one successful person who may be their friend, I see them living in the moment, driving someone else's car, eating for free and crashing at their friend's pad. If the friend's fortune changes so does theirs because they have never bothered to pursue their own dreams or work for what they want.

I still see the relevance of this lesson every passing day. By the way, he eventually gave me the car a few years later, practically forcing it on me urging me to invest my money in other worthwhile ventures.

Prosperity is a great teacher; adversity a greater.

William Hazlitt

I learn nothing was more important than his family as he chose to go without so others didn't have to.

In 1996, daddy exhibited the greatest love anyone could show to his mother. By then he had retired and he needed to send money to the village for his mother's upkeep and unfortunately he didn't have it. He consulted me but sadly I was also low on funds as well so I didn't reply on time. I was hoping to send him some money at the end of the month when I got paid.

He wrote another letter to me saying I should not worry if I didn't have the money and that the alternative was for him to sell his car because he wouldn't live to see the day his mother had to go hungry or beg for food.

When I got the letter, I wept bitterly because I was unable to meet a need that daddy had. It was as though God knew, or more like read my heart, as later that afternoon I had to go on a two-day business trip.

I worked really hard to ensure I could complete the computer installation project in one day, which enabled me to have enough money left (I was given a set fee) to deliver the project and I saved on cost by finishing quicker than planned, avoiding an extra night's cost in the hotel.

As soon as I landed back at the airport, I caught a bus and travelled to see my father, but more importantly to give him the money, which I knew he was desperate for.

It was a big relief for me and I was excited to put a smile on his face. It wasn't the fact that daddy wanted to sell his car that bothered me but the fact that he was ready to go the extra mile to make his mother happy.

He was the same way with his children as well. He would sacrifice anything to make us happy. When other fathers would consider the meat in their meal as something to relish, daddy would eat the meal and leave the meat for my sister and I. He would sit and watch us devour it and that gave him all the satisfaction and joy he needed.

When I look back now, I think of my poor mum putting the best cuts of meat on my daddy's plate knowing fully well that it would end up in us.

My brother shared this story with me as one of the lessons that struck a chord with him and I decided to share it in his own words. Through his story, I learnt about a father who was willing to sell his only car to ensure his mother's monthly upkeep was not impacted by the delay in his pension payment.

Love is that condition in which the happiness of another person is essential to your own.

Robert Heinlein

I am the good shepherd. The good shepherd lays down his life for the sheep.

John 10:11

My brother and I learn he would protect us no matter what the cost.

It was one of those rare moments that mum and dad had a misunderstanding. The amazing thing was that daddy and mummy shielded us from those times so that we never got to know.

This particular time, daddy moved from the master bedroom to the room my brother and I shared. He told us to swap rooms and he moved his clothes to our room. We were too young to read any meaning to it so it didn't seem like a big deal to us; after all we were crashing next to mum.

A couple of days later mummy called my brother and I and asked us to go and find out from daddy why he left their bedroom.

That very day, daddy was in our room having his afternoon nap. The room was relatively dark as the curtains were drawn. He saw us come into the room so my brother and I leaned our backs against the wall beside the door and slid down to a sitting position. He asked us what the matter was.

Generally I was more vocal than my brother, never afraid to say anything. So he started nudging me with his elbow, urging me to speak.

Eventually I asked, "Daddy, why did you leave your room?"

Instead of answering the question, he got up briskly from the bed, started packing his belongings and asked us to help him move them back to the master bedroom.

He never discussed anything with us but he moved back to his room and everything went back to normal. As much as possible, daddy and mummy shielded any misunderstanding they had from us.

This meant we grew up feeling safe and secure as a family. The thought of growing up without both of them never occurred to us. Our house was peaceful as we never witnessed a row, slammed doors or raised voices. We knew there were occasional tense moments but they were so few and far between that we never had to worry as children.

That is a precious gift to children; I know it was to us.

Let them shout for joy and be glad, who favour my righteous cause. Yes, let them say continually, "The Lord be magnified, who has pleasure in the prosperity of his servant!"

Psalm 35:27

I learn that a set back does not have to define you and anyone can recover from a disappointment.

One lesson that stands out for me was on the back of a little disappointment.

I was in a school where I was able to compete with my peers and no one took the first position from me while I was there. At year-end, two students were picked from each school to do a special exam, to gain admission into a federal government college. This is like gaining admission to an elite school, where children of high-ranking government officials, politicians and the wealthy would end up being your classmates.

I was among a number of students that were to take the exams. Other parents were informed but for whatever reason, the teacher did not inform my father. I never bothered to tell him either as I just assumed he knew.

On the day of the examination, on a Saturday morning, I told my daddy that I was suppose to write the exam today but daddy was shocked and said no. I guess he felt he never prepared me for the exam. The following Monday morning, daddy went directly to the head-teacher's office to complain.

He wanted to know why he was not informed that I was suppose to sit the exam and frustratingly he told them that, with or without the exams, I would pass my common entrance examination and would be able to compete with the students who got the opportunity to do so.

The result came out and I guess those students that were allowed to write the examinations did not pass so no one went to the elite school. It was then that my class teacher told daddy that not informing him was a conspiracy between the head teacher and some of the other teachers. There were supposed to be two students from each school and for whatever reasons, they were hand picked by the head teacher.

Daddy called me, sat me down and told me I would go to another college called Titcombe and that I must prove to my so-called teachers, that with or without the elite school I would make it.

He made me believe in myself and his words kept ringing in my ears, "YOU MUST BE SOMEBODY IN LIFE".

My sister told me this story fondly and I knew it was worth sharing because everyone deserves to know that a setback or a disappointing does not define us.

People seldom improve when they have no other model but themselves to copy.

Oliver Goldsmith

I learn not to give up on people and to always help them discover and pursue their potential.

I have to tell the story of a boy whose parent lived down the street. He was my sister's very good friend but he was also a tout, a real bad boy and his parents had lost hope in him.

They had tried all they could to make him somebody in life but he was always getting into trouble. It was so bad, that sometimes the police would arrest his parents because it was the only way they could get to him or get him to turn himself in.

He dropped out of school and, at that point, my sister stopped being his friend. One day his mother came in to my mum's shop and she saw my father outside offering advice to someone. I think his reputation at the time as the 'grand life coach' had preceded him. She fell on her knees telling him all she had gone through with regard to the boy, all the while weeping bitterly.

Daddy consoled her and asked her to believe in God and in the boy for once, and then he asked to see him. My sister's friend, or more like ex-friend, came round to our house that evening to see daddy and they hit it off. The relationship strengthened to the point that he would regularly come by to see daddy and he loved to hang around at our house.

Initially she thought he liked coming because he was taking a shine to her but she was wrong. My father had started talking to him regularly and he was fast becoming a part of our family. As time went by, he left some of his friends because most of the time he was at our place and no longer had time to hang out with the bad crowd.

The more time he spent with my father, the more he became discontent with his life and future. He came round and ate quite a few meals with dad who, in turn, took the opportunity to advise him.

One day he told daddy he wanted to join the army and he encouraged him; he collected the form, did the exams, passed and joined the army.

The day he came to see us in his uniform, daddy was overwhelmed with joy and tears rolled down his face. Seeing a young man that people had lost hope in becoming someone in life was more than anyone could handle without tears in their eyes. The boy wept too. I guess he knew more than anyone that his life could have ended very differently.

The last time my sister saw him, a few years later, he told her about his plans of furthering his education. We had so much pride and joy in our hearts seeing the transformation in him and the role played by our father in his transformation. I am so sure he will forever remember daddy for his contribution to his life.

Daddy never believed that there was anyone who could not make it in life. He saw the potential in everyone and never gave up trying to help the person find and achieve it.

"Put it before them briefly so they will read it, clearly so they will appreciate it, picturesquely so they will remember it and, above all, accurately so they will be guided by its light."

Pulitzer, Joseph

Closing Remarks

The idea to write a book about the lessons we all learnt from my father was one that came from me sharing some lessons with friends.

The more I shared, the more I realised there was more to share. I hope these stories have been a blessing to you as you've walked this journey with me.

Olayemi A. Adelekan

Printed in Poland
by Amazon Fulfillment
Poland Sp. z o.o., Wrocław